ATTACK YOUR DAY!

Before It Attacks You

TRAPPER WOODS | MARK WOODS

NEW YORK

Attack Your Day! Before It Attacks You

by Trapper Woods and Mark Woods.
© 2011 Trapper Woods and Mark Woods. All rights reserved.

ISBN 978-160037-848-5 (Paperback)

Published by:

Morgan James Publishing
5 Penn Plaza, 23rd Floor
New York City, New York 10001
(212) 655-5470 Office
(516) 908-4496 Fax
www.MorganJamesPublishing.com

Cover Design by: Daniel Krieger

In an effort to support local communities, raise awareness and funds, Morgan James Publishing donates one percent of all book sales for the life of each book to Habitat for Humanity. Get involved today, visit **www.HelpHabitatForHumanity.org.**

DEDICATION

To my father Trapper Woods (1935-2010) who taught me that time is our most precious commodity. That in life, it is the relationships we forge and simple moments in time that matter most.

ACKNOWLEDGEMENTS

The authors wish to thank their family, friends, and colleagues for their encouragement and commitment to the development of this book. A special thanks to, William A. Guillory, Brenda Woods, Becky Harding, and Paul Woods for the diamond story.

www.attackyourday.com

INTRODUCTION

In 1986, I changed my career. I joined Dr. Charles R. Hobbs to be one of his Time Power seminar facilitators. I was fortunate to have Charles as a mentor. Charles was a leader in time management strategies and a major influence in initiating the time management training wave which continues even today. His Time Power seminar has become a classic and continues to have life-changing impact on its practitioners, including me. The Time Power seminar is still the backbone of our training business.

When Charles sold his company to Day-Timer, Inc., I was invited to work directly for Day-Timer at their corporate offices in Allentown, PA. Serving as a consultant to and for Day-Timer further solidified my interest in the subject of time. Through the Day-Timer connection, I had the opportunity of talking time with hundreds of corporations and organizations.

I later started my own consulting firm and, shortly thereafter, met William A. Guillory, PhD. Bill invited me to co-author the book *Tick Tock Who Broke the Clock?* with him, and we became friends. Bill, a scientist and gifted educator, challenged me and helped me in numerous ways. I used to joke, "He makes me think so hard I always have a headache after we've been together." Bill's ideas have been a major influence in the development of this book.

In 1998 my son, Mark, began providing a consulting service to my company. It was Mark who patiently led us through the technology wilderness and into the 21st century. Mark is co-author and a major contributor to this book. His Generation X-perspective has been immeasurably helpful.

We now find ourselves swimming in a cyber sea, filled with unbelievable technology. We have BlackBerrys, Strawberries, iPods, Pea Pods, iPhones and killer Droids, Facebook's latest looks, and the glitter of all that twitter. Yet, people still can't manage their time. After twenty-three years as a time management consultant, logging over two and a half million miles in the air, training many thousands of individuals, I figured it was about time Mark and I wrote this book . . . about time.

So here is a quick-fix approach to time management that doesn't take more time to learn than the amount of time it saves.

Trapper Woods, FatherTime™

TABLE OF CONTENTS

Chapter I

ACTIVITIES RULE!
NOT THE CLOCK
Don't Be a Slave to Time

So you've read all the best-selling books about time management and productivity. They sounded good at first. In fact, they are good. But, you didn't implement them, or implemented them only for a short time, because they seemed to further complicate an already complicated world. It's hard to remember what all those principles and skills are, let alone apply them. The problem with some of the old, established time management strategies is many of them do not fit today's high-intensity, rapidly changing and fast-paced environment.

What we need today are fast, flexible, and ridiculously easy solutions to help us navigate "time" for greater productivity.

Is there an easier way to approach the time challenges we face today in this chaotic world? We think so!

You already know what the problem is: Times have changed. Not that time itself has changed; it hasn't. But, the times in which we live have changed. It's not that we don't have enough time—we have the same amount of time we've always had, and all the time we ever will have.

The problem is that we have more events and activities to manage in the same amount of time. This is due, in part, to technology, the Internet and expectations of doing more with less. We are wired 24 hours a day, 7 days a week, 365 days a year, with multiple demands, and hardly a chance to catch our breath. In a way, we've become compressors of life, trying to jam an unrealistic number of events into our daily allotment of minutes.

All of this has caused a paradigm shift. A paradigm is a patterned way of thinking. The old way of thinking had us dividing our work and personal life with an imaginary line. For most people, that simply doesn't work anymore. For some people it never worked, simply because life was too complicated. When we separate work and personal life with an imaginary line, we set the two up in opposition to each other. That drives stress upward. We feel guilty regardless of which side of the line is getting our attention.

The new paradigm is for us to see our work and personal life as one life, with work and personal activities integrated throughout the 24-hour day.

Maybe you're thinking that an integrated work and personal life sounds undesirable. Maybe, for you, it even sounds as final as placing the last nail in the coffin of work-life balance. After all, doesn't work-life balance mean equally dividing time between work and personal life? No, that's the old way of thinking.

The new way of thinking about *balance* is to realize it means maintaining equilibrium in a sea of change. It requires the ability to *flexicute*. Okay, so we invented a word—but, you have to agree, it is a very descriptive word and it makes sense. *Flexicuting* activities, means the ability to adapt to changes during the day without letting it throw you. It is executing activities by way of being flexible. As author James Ballard said, "We need to learn to dance while the carpet is being pulled from underneath us."

The first step in creating ridiculously easy time management is to learn the new "time management dance steps." In other words, recognize and embrace the simple but significant differences in the new time paradigm.

Here are some old ways of operating as compared to the new ways. Making these adjustments will help you be more comfortable with chaos.

Old way: Balance meant equal amounts of time spent on work and personal life.

New way: Balance is maintaining equilibrium in a sea of change.

Old way: Emphasis on multi-tasking.

New way: Emphasis on alternate-tasking, alternating work and personal life activities around the clock in a way in which both can be fully experienced.

Old way: Work is a marathon with long, hard hours and inadequate recovery time.

New way: Work is a series of sprints with adequate recovery time. (Source: *The Power of Full Engagement* by Jim Loehr and Tony Schwartz.)

Old way: After-hours accessibility was limited.

New way: All-hours accessibility is becoming standard with technology.

Old way: Daily schedules and plans were fixed.

New way: Daily schedules and plans are fluid and flexible.

Old way: Work could be caught up and finished.

New way: Work is continuously processed but seldom finished.

Old way: One time management tool provided a complete system.

New way: Multiple tools are combined to provide a complete system.

Old way: Activities were arranged primarily based upon the clock.

New way: Activities arranged primarily based upon necessity, practicality, efficiency, and spontaneity. In other words, doing activities when they make sense, rather than based on what time it is.

Old way: Performance is judged by the number of hours one puts in at the office.

New way: Performance is judged on the basis of productivity.

Let's emphasize again that time hasn't changed. We still measure time by the same calendar and clock.

And, time is still defined as the occurrence of events one after another. An event is anything that happens, including activities: these are the basic building blocks for designing the quality of life we desire.

Activities Rule

In the new paradigm, the clock does not rule: activities rule. If you are looking for an easier way to manage time, it is simply to become an effective activity manager.

Let's take a closer look at the nature of activities, as outlined in the book *Tick Tock Who Broke the Clock? – Solving the Work-Life Balance Equation*, co-authored by Dr. William A. Guillory and Trapper Woods.

An activity is something we do. Even sleeping is an activity. From the day we draw our first breath of life until the time we expire our last breath of life, we are executing activities on a nonstop basis. Examining activities further, we realize that activities can be:

- Physical

- Mental

- Subliminal

- Long in duration

- Short in duration

Activities Are Never Neutral

Some activities of long duration can have very little consequence. Some activities of short duration can have huge consequences. The most important thing to recognize about activities is that they are never neutral. They either enhance or detract from our lives by changing the quality for better or for worse. The following statements illustrate this point:

- Activities that align with what we value give us a greater sense of satisfaction than those that don't.

- Activities creatively arranged in a sequence can culminate in the achievement of a desired outcome or goal.

- Negative activities repeated over and over again can erode our well-being.

- Positive activities repeated over and over again can make us stronger and improve our well-being.

- Activities repeated over and over again become habits. Habits can be our greatest servants or our worst masters.

- When we choose to do certain activities we simultaneously exclude other activities. It's about choice.

- We can change the quality of our life simply by changing activities.

- Focus permits us to fully experience an activity.

- The day's productivity is determined by the activities we choose and those we refuse.

- We live and die with our choice of activities.

To Be a High Performer

Hopefully you feel empowered with a better understanding of activities. The exciting thing here is that to be good at what you want to be good at—to be a high producer in today's environment—simply be a good activity chooser. It's easy! Poor choosers become losers when competing for promotions or getting what they want in life. The bottom line is this—self-management excellence is really activity management excellence.

Three Incredible Gifts

Getting down to the most basic of basics, you need to realize that each day we are given three incredible gifts.

They are:

✓ The gift of *time*, without which activities cannot be executed.

✓ The gift of personal *energy* essential for doing the activities.

✓ The gift of *choice* to determine what activities we will do.

To maximize these three amazing daily gifts, the following activity management skills must be implemented:

1. Choosing activities

2. Tracking activities

3. Arranging activities

4. Flexicuting activities

5. Focusing on activities

ATTACK YOUR DAY!

This ridiculously easy time management approach is to simply get good at these five activity management skills. We're going to forget about all the old laws and rules, and just focus on becoming good activity managers.

These skills will help you stress less, avoid overwhelm, and deal with interruptions so you can enjoy life. It's time to color your choices.

Chapter 2

COLOR YOUR CHOICES
The Art of Choosing and Refusing

The first essential skill of activity management is to be a good *chooser*. Activity management is really just *choice* management, *option* management and *decision* management. The investment of time is always about this activity or that activity, and choosing what to do next. The best managers are really just excellent activity choosers. Those who experience the work-life quality and balance they desire are skillful activity choosers.

Get What You Want

Get what you want out of life. You can have it or not, based on your activity choices.

A key part of choosing activities is refusing activities. Good choosers are also good refusers. They know how to say no. One of the first steps to overwhelm is the inability to say no to activities that distract from value-added activities. Put another way, overcoming overwhelm is all about saying no.

Most people think saying no involves only saying no to others. The real gist of saying no is being able to say no to your self. There is always the temptation to say yes to activities that are fast, activities that are fun, activities that are familiar, activities that are easy and instantly rewarding. It's so much easier to clean the kitchen sink than to balance the checkbook. We sometimes even welcome interruptions as an excuse for procrastinating on activities we really don't want to do.

When we choose instant-reward activities at the expense of value-added activities, our productivity goes down and very often some self-esteem with it. When we do this, we put ourselves into our very own choice-made activity trap. If we do this habitually, we begin to get a bigger and bigger backlog of value-added activities that need to be done, which, as you may well imagine, drives stress up . . . way up! That's right! Full-blown overwhelm! To avoid this, it is critical to learn when, where, and how to say no to yourself!

Making great choices, knowing what activities to choose and what to refuse, begins by taking the long view. The long view is deciding what you want to occur in the future, and then specifying the activities required to make it a reality. Your future is any time beyond today.

This means creating a crystal clear picture of the outcomes you desire to produce with the activities you plan to execute. Just doing activities without a destination in mind is like spinning your wheels on an icy road. You are burning energy but not going anywhere.

Pre-determine and Anticipate

The process to use to avoid spinning your wheels is quite simple. First, you need to pre-determine outcomes; next, anticipate the activities required to produce the outcomes. The most important step is to then decide which activities need to be done today and do them.

Humans are wired to follow this exact process. Think about it. Either consciously or sub-consciously, we say to ourselves all day long, "What will I do next?" We then choose a desired outcome followed by the execution of activities that will make it occur. Much has been written about this simple process. It's called goal setting.

Goal setting actually intimidates some people, but it shouldn't. We are, by nature, designed to:

• Create a mental picture of what we want.

- Make a plan of the activities required to get those results. (This is what we refer to as building an activity path.)

- Do the activities we've planned.

What we are saying is that it is impossible to be a good activity chooser without first glancing into the future and visualizing the results you want.

Once you put this process in motion, you will not be like people who spin their wheels at work. People who do spin their wheels at work are on the slippery slope of indecisiveness, and indecisiveness is the enemy of getting started. Similar to a car in neutral, one which can't go anywhere until it's in gear, indecisiveness puts you in neutral time.

What's the best way to stop wheel spinning and get in gear? First, take time to create clarity of purpose or a clear understanding of your desired results. Define very specifically the results you want. Clarity is the mother of decisiveness, and is the reason for the activities you choose and execute. The skill of making effectual choices starts with this process. Here is a simple, real-life example:

- The mental picture of the desired result is:

  o Playing tennis with my friend Todd at 10:00 a.m. Saturday morning at the Fairmont Park Courts.

- The activities required to make this happen include:

  o Pick up the phone and make the date with Todd.

  o Call and reserve court time.

  o Buy tennis balls.

  o Leave for the courts at 9:30 a.m. on Saturday morning.

Isn't that easy? You are wired to think and act this way by nature. You couldn't get anything done without this process. It's ridiculously easy.

Create, Then Do

Here's proof you don't need an expert to teach you how to set and achieve goals—you, yourself, are already an expert. You already do it every day of your life. You *create* a mental picture of the desired results (for instance, that you want to play tennis at 10 a.m. Saturday morning) and then you *do* the pictures. In other words, do the activities (make the appointment, schedule the court time, etc.) or take the steps necessary to get you to that desired result.

We've used this simple example to show you how you use this process every day without even realizing it. This process always works—whether it's something as ridiculously easy as setting a tennis date or as complex as setting a career path goal.

People who do not have clear pictures of what they want in their lives automatically default their futures to the possibility of undesirable outcomes. They, in effect, leave their lives to chance or the "fickle finger of fate." Ultimately, they see themselves as victims of the unfairness of life.

Once clarity of future outcomes is established, it is then possible to choose and refuse daily activities to insure choices that produce results.

Color Your Choices

We must become highly skillful at managing our daily activity traffic. Just as with heavy traffic on a freeway, our daily activity traffic congests our day. It makes it difficult for us to move forward with our plans. We are often forced to take detours away from our desired direction.

Like automobile traffic, our daily activity traffic can be controlled by a metaphorical traffic light. The traffic light will help us be better at the second part of being good activity choosers. Simply put, activity traffic management requires the ability to know when to stop, when to go, when to use caution, and when to say no.

We assigned the colors of the traffic light to the three types of activities we deal with every single day: Red, Green, and Yellow. We added Gray as a forth type. Yes, we know there isn't a gray light, but use your imagination.

STOP! Do Now

Red means stop whatever you are doing and go do the red activity right this minute. Now! Red activities are high payoff and urgent (meaning they require immediate action). Some examples of red activities are: the network is down, an accident, equipment breakdown, project deadline, unscheduled meeting, customer complaint, sick child at home, or a sudden demand from the boss. These are no-brainer choices. When they occur, we must respond.

GO! The Majority of Your Day

Our activity traffic also includes green activities. Green stands for go! Go and do green activities as much as possible. Do as many green activities in a day as you can. Green activities do not require an immediate response (in other words, they're not urgent), but be aware that many green activities can become red activities if we don't do them when we should.

Green is where the money is made. Green is where relationships are nurtured. Green is where we learn and grow and become our best selves. Green activities help us balance our work and our personal life. Green activities are high payoff, value-added activities. Green activities include daily planning, family time, building business relationships, training, exercise, long-range planning, reading, hiking, running, cleaning, shopping, time with friends and virtually every activity that promotes our personal and professional well-being.

CAUTION! Really

Yellow activities do not require immediate action and are not value-added activities, but they may have some degree of lesser value. But beware! Sometimes yellow activities come to us wrapped in the context of artificial urgency, like when an associate drops in and claims our help is needed right now. One of the challenges of modern technology is that it can create counterfeit urgency. An email or instant message announced with a beep or an alarm on your cell phone signaling a text message or missed call are examples of how some messages get our attention and seem urgent when often they really are not urgent at all. Nevertheless, we are tempted to respond to these counterfeit urgencies.

When yellow activities, disguised as urgencies, clamor for our attention, remember that yellow means caution. Yellow activities can and should be rescheduled for a later time, a time that is more appropriate. When we recognize a yellow activity, we need to reschedule it and proceed with what we were doing. Failure to do this puts us in a state of illusion. Oh, yes. We are busy all right, but probably spending time on activities of dubious value during our heavily congested day. Example of Yellow activities includes: purging email, office filing, expense report, planning vacation, paying bills, or scheduling a doctor appointment. Yellow activities needs to be done, but not today, tomorrow, or maybe even next week.

NO! Don't Even Think About It

Gray activities are a complete waste of time. Don't waste "gray matter" on gray activities. Just say no! If we are honest with ourselves, we all know what these are—a few examples include: gossip, junk mail, negativity, complaining, etc. Remember what we said earlier: the inability to say no is the first step to overwhelm.

The payoff for being skillful at choosing and refusing is huge. People who are good at it always have a leg up on the corporate ladder. It's one of the most important survival skills in modern organizations today.

Mother Knew Best

It's actually easy to make some sense out of our daily activity traffic. We merely need to follow the advice of our mothers, "Eat your greens." Stay away from the starchy yellow and gray activities that have very little productivity value. Managing our daily activity traffic this way can facilitate our making fast and good choices. Ridiculously easy time management, is about making good choices.

You can begin today to color your activity choices. Then, manage your choices with the metaphorical traffic light. You'll make great choices that way. You'll always know when to stop, when to go, when to use caution by rescheduling, and when to say no. Don't be colorblind. See every activity in the context of its true color.

Chapter 3

CARRY YOUR TIME IN BUCKETS
Fine-Tune Your Tools

The next crucial self-management skill is activity tracking. This involves keeping track of intangible things such as thoughts, ideas, talking points, dates, promises, reminders, and strategies.

These intangible things must be organized and tracked so nothing falls through the cracks. This is especially crucial in this era of information overload. This is where the right time/activity management tools come in.

Time management tools today are innovative, clever, and even astounding. In some cases, they are also very expensive. The selection from which to choose is huge and includes both electronic devices and paper planners. So, the questions are, "What kinds of tools are best for you and your lifestyle?" "Should you use a paper planner, an electronic planner or a combination of paper and electronic devices?"

I was flying on a commuter jet one morning. Sitting across the aisle from me was an obviously effective executive. She had a palm computer in one hand and a cell phone in the other. I thought to myself: if ever there was an executive who was totally paperless, it just might be this woman.

When we leveled off at 10,000 feet, I thought, "Now I bet she'll take out a laptop," but not so. She took out a paper Day-Timer® Organizer. I introduced myself and asked, "How come? Why do you use a paper planner when you are so good with electronic tools?" She said, "Well, there are many things in my business that don't track well electronically. That's why I augment my electronic systems with paper."

Keep It Simple

Many people operate this way. They use a combination of paper and electronic. Others operate strictly with a paper planner, and some are electronic only. The key is to keep it simple. If you combine tools, you should be sure they don't duplicate functions. For example, don't try to operate on two calendars.

Let's face it: time management tools do not manage time. People manage time. The tools are designed for one thing. They help us track the events and activities that are crucial to us.

Here is an easy way to think of and use time/ activity management tools. Think of them as buckets. A bucket is used to collect and carry things. Paper planners, palm computers and smartphones contain buckets in which we collect and carry data and plans for activities and events.

To ensure nothing falls through the cracks, we suggest you always carry six buckets, which are essential for effective time/activity management.

Bucket One — The Monthly Calendar

Bucket one is the monthly bucket or, in other words, your monthly calendar. Monthly calendars can be paper or electronic. (**See Figure 1** for an example of a typical paper monthly calendar.) It is for collecting and carrying future events and scheduled activities. You've likely been using a monthly calendar this way for years.

If you've known an event or activity was going to occur on some future date, you simply wrote it on your calendar on that future date. Nothing hard about that!

Figure 1

Bucket One — The Monthly Calendar

© Day-Timer, Inc.

However, many people do not use their calendar as effectively as they could. It is critical they do, though, because bucket number one, the monthly calendar, is like a master control panel. It's the one place we can go and quickly see all of our scheduled future commitments, both personal and business.

To maximize the power of bucket one, and to ensure it really is your master control panel, use the monthly calendar for **ADD**. We aren't talking about Attention Deficit Disorder here. We are talking about all:

✓ **A**ppointments, and all

✓ **D**ates, and all

✓ **D**eadlines

The Most Important Appointment

Let's consider appointment activities for a moment. When scheduling appointments, remember the most important appointments you ever schedule on your calendar will be the appointments you schedule with yourself.

Take a look at your calendar for the past few months. Have you made any appointments with yourself and honored them the same way you treat your appointments with others? If not, you are not taking advantage of one of the most beneficial calendaring techniques.

What is the objective of self-appointments? They are for solitary focus time when you can accomplish your green activities. People who expect this kind of time to materialize without scheduling it usually come up short.

In the new time integration paradigm, we suggest that both business and personal appointments go on the same calendar. Some people attempt to use two different calendars, which increases the likelihood of losing control.

Dates and deadlines are also crucial in making your monthly calendar a master control panel. Many people fail to put deadlines on their calendar. Some people don't keep their calendars current and they become unreliable. If you want time management to be ridiculously easy, keep your calendar current.

Select a paper or electronic calendar that you will be willing to carry with you. Like a wrist watch, accessibility of your calendar is essential in today's mobile and virtual work environment. Take it to meetings. Have it with you when you go to confer in another person's office. Invariably, you'll be contacted all day long by others asking for some of your time. If you have bucket one accessible, you won't have to get back to people.

Please take a moment now and evaluate your effectiveness in using a monthly calendar. My monthly calendar for future events and activities that are scheduled is:

_____ Paper

_____ Electronic

_____ Don't use one

My effectiveness rating is:

0   1   2   3   4   5   6   7   8   9   10

Not	Somewhat	Highly
Effective	Effective	Effective

Bucket Two — The Catch-All Bucket

Bucket two is the catch-all bucket. (**See Figure 2** for an example.) It is similar to the monthly calendar bucket in that it's a place to hold future events and activities. The difference is that the future events and activities in the catch-all bucket have yet to be scheduled. In other words, you know you are going to do these things in the future, but you aren't exactly sure when. Certainly you won't do them today, probably not tomorrow, and maybe not even next week. The catch-all bucket gives you a good place to track these things so they won't be forgotten.

Figure 2
Bucket Two — The Catch-All Bucket

ITEM NO	NUMBER EACH ITEM	ITEM NO	NUMBER EACH ITEM
	TO BE DONE IN JUNE		

June

S	M	T	W	T	F	S
		1	2	3	4	5
6	7	8	9	10	11	12
13	14	15	16	17	18	19
20	21	22	23	24	25	26
27	28	29	30			

July

S	M	T	W	T	F	S
				1	2	3	4
5	6	7	8	9	10	11
12	13	14	15	16	17	18
19	20	21	22	23	24	25
26	27	28	29	30	31	

© Day-Timer, Inc.

For some paper planners, the catch-all bucket is on the back of the monthly calendars, entitled "To Be Done." You can also set up an electronic catch-all bucket, or you can designate some sort of journal for that purpose.

It's easy to spot people who don't have a catch-all bucket. Their pockets, handbags, and desk tops are usually cluttered with little pieces of paper on which they carry vital information. They can often be seen frantically searching for that one piece of paper with the information they need at that moment.

We believe bucket number two is almost as essential as bucket number one. This bucket exists for RAM. We aren't talking about your computer's **RAM** here; we are talking about **R**eminders, **A**voiding FPAA, and **M**aster Task List.

- **R**eminders. People have so much to remember it is difficult to track it all in our minds. Anytime you want to remember anything, just put it in your catch-all bucket.

- **A**voiding FPAA. That's an acronym for Floating Paper Anxiety Attack! We think you know we're talking about. We get caught in a situation without something to write on, so we grab any old piece of paper to capture an important message. Then, for some reason, that paper gets lost or floats away, and up goes our anxiety because it contained very important information.

o I've watched people make important notes on napkins, business cards, pieces of yellow legal paper, wallpaper, yellow stickies, and even seen people write on the palm of their hand.

We were conducting a time management seminar in Oklahoma City one day. When we started talking about floating paper, the manager of the group stood up and said, "Hey! Do you mean like this?" and he pulled two big wads of paper out of his trouser pockets. We said, "Yes, like that! That's a complicated way to track events and activities."

If you want ridiculously easy time management, have one catch-all bucket where you put all the information that's handed to you on floating pieces of paper. It takes just seconds to transcribe the information. Then, throw the little bits and pieces of paper away. Life will be amazingly simpler, and you'll have less anxiety.

• Master Task List. Everybody has a list of stuff they need to remember to do each month. The catch-all bucket is a place to build a summary of such things.

o For example: before the end of the month, you want to purge your files. Put that in your catch-all bucket. You won't forget it, and you'll increase the likelihood it will get done.

WARNING! A catch-all bucket is not much help at all unless it is checked each morning as part of the planning process. It takes very little time to scan the information. Please take a moment and evaluate your effectiveness using a catch-all bucket.

My catch-all bucket for future events and activities that are not yet scheduled is:

_____ Paper

_____ Electronic

_____ Don't use one

My effectiveness rating is:

0   1   2   3   4   5   6   7   8   9   10

Not   Somewhat   Highly
Effective   Effective   Effective

Bucket Three — The Daily Bucket

Bucket three is a bucket for today's activities. **(See Figure 3** for an example.) We call it the **AAA** bucket. And, as you may well have guessed, we aren't talking about the American Automobile Association.

We are talking about:

✓ **A**ppointments: today's appointments

✓ **A**ction list: today's activity list or to-do's

✓ **A**dditions: things that pop up

Almost all paper and electronic planners have a space for today's appointments and action list. Bucket three functions like a compass. It shows us what we plan to do next. It shows us where we are headed and what we've scheduled to be doing at certain times. It also provides a place for us to note the "expected/unexpected" things that pop up during the day— the additions.

CARRY YOUR TIME IN BUCKETS

Figure 3
Bucket Three — The Daily Bucket

MONDAY
26 JUNE

188 Days Left

MAY / JUNE / JULY (calendar grid)

TO BE DONE TODAY (ACTION LIST)

APPOINTMENTS & SCHEDULED EVENTS

HOURS · NAME · PLACE · SUBJECT

7 0700
8 0800
9 0900
10 1000
11 1100
12 1200
1 1300
2 1400
3 1500
4 1600
5 1700
6 1800
7 1900
8 2000
9 2100
10 2200

PHONE CALLS

EXPENSE & REIMBURSEMENT RECORD

© Day-Timer, Inc.

-33-

Most people are pretty good at having a place to track their appointments for the day. We are concerned, however, when we see people who don't take the time to make a simple action list for the day. Interestingly, some time management experts tell their clients it doesn't make sense to plan an action list at the beginning of the day because things change so fast. Their argument is that the plan might be obsolete as early as 8:00 or 9:00 in the morning, so that kind of planning is a waste of time. We disagree with that idea.

When we build a list of planned activities for the day, an action list, and we put a value on those activities, four incredible benefits accrue to the ridiculously effective activity manager.

Three benefits are still there even when things change and the list becomes obsolete when interruptions occur. Here are four HUGE benefits:

1. The list becomes a tool of negotiation. It can be used as a tool of negotiation with yourself when you are tempted to be swayed by lower priorities. It can also be used as a tool of negotiation with others when they want you to subordinate your priorities to theirs.

2. It becomes a tool of navigation to help you get back on track after you've dealt with emergencies—red events you had to resolve.

3. It becomes a tool of focus because it functions like a magnifying glass to help you concentrate your physical, mental, and emotional energy on the right activities throughout the day.

4. It becomes a tool of measurement to help you evaluate your progress during the day, and shows the status of each planned activity at the end of the day.

Why would anybody want to run headlong into the whitewater of the day without an action list when it produces such benefits?

What do we mean by additions? Additions are the "expected/unexpected" activities and events that pop up each day after we've made our plan. They are the red events in our daily traffic that require us to stop what we are doing, or what we planned to do, and go do this red event right now! We think there is worth to adding these to our original action list, and taking credit for getting those jobs done by checking them off.

Please take a moment and evaluate your effectiveness using your daily bucket.

My daily bucket used for today's events and activities is:

_____ Paper

_____ Electronic

_____ Don't use one consistently

My effectiveness rating is:

0   1   2   3   4   5   6   7   8   9   10

Not   Somewhat   Highly
Effective   Effective   Effective

Bucket Four — The Memory Bucket

Bucket four is the memory bucket. It's the place for **DDT**. Clearly, we are not talking about pesticide here. We are talking about:

✓ **D**ocumenting important information

✓ **D**elegating to and receiving delegation from others

✓ **T**racking a sequence of events and information you receive

It's where we record important information that comes to us during the day—information which we think we might need at a later date. During the day, we receive information in a variety of ways. It comes to us through telephone calls, drop-in visitors, email, voicemail, text messages, meetings and conversations with others. We certainly don't write everything down, but recording key information is crucial.

What we are talking about here is a permanent journal that is dated, sequential, and ultimately archived in such a way that you can retrieve the information, if necessary, years from the date it was recorded.

Choose the best tool that fits your style. All tools, paper, or electronic, have resources that you can use as "buckets."

(See Figure 4 on page 38 for an example of a memory bucket.)

ATTACK YOUR DAY!

Figure 4
Bucket Four — The Memory Bucket

DIARY AND WORK RECORD	26th Week 177th Day	**MONDAY** JUNE	**26**

REF.	NAME OR PROJECT	DETAILS OF MEETINGS • AGREEMENTS • DECISIONS	TIME HRS. 1/10
1			
2			
3			
4			
5			
6			
7			
8			
9			
10			
11			
12			
13			
14			
15			
16			
17			
18			
19			
20			
21			
22			
23			
24			
25			
26			
27			
28			
29			
30			
31			
32			
33			
34			
35			
36			
37			
38			
39			
40			

REFILL #92804

DESK TWO PAGE PER DAY REFERENCE

© Day-Timer, Inc.

People who don't use bucket four, the memory bucket, often resort to writing on legal pads, spiral notebooks and loose pieces of paper. This can be risky. Remember this old Chinese proverb: "The palest ink is better than the best memory." However, what you write down can't be used as memory at all unless you have a good retrieval system for finding the information.

Because retrieval is so important, we recommend to all PDA users (as well as paper planner users) that the memory bucket be paper, with the day's date printed on each page. Then you can file these pages sequentially.

If you want to experience ridiculously easy time management, settle on a dated paper journal for your memory bucket and use it consistently. Lack of consistency with this tool will make your time management harder, not easier.

Please take a moment and evaluate your effectiveness using a memory bucket that is sequential and dated.

My memory bucket used for recording key information is:

_____ Paper

_____ Electronic

_____ Don't use one

SWITCH TO ELECTRONIC for SEARCH MODE

My effectiveness rating is:

0   1   2   3   4   5   6   7   8   9   10

Not   Somewhat   Highly
Effective   Effective   Effective

Bucket Five — The Data Bucket

Tracking bucket five is the data bucket. This is where we carry vital information that we need at our fingertips from time to time, and might include goals, projects, an address and telephone directory, fact sheets, etc.

The purpose of the data bucket is to centralize the information we need at our fingertips. To centralize means to get all of our key information into one source. When we do that, we promote ridiculously easy time management.

One of the huge advantages of a PDA such as a Blackberry, iPhone, Palm, and Android™ is that you can download all of your data from your computer into a very small data bucket that you carry in the palm of your hand. If you do not use a PDA, but instead use a paper planner, a tabbed index section serves as your data bucket. We also want to note that some people use Outlook, while others use CRM software programs like Salesforce.com, Sage

ACT!, Landslide, and ZOHO. You can learn more about data bucket tools and find additional resources online at our website attackyourday.com.

Please evaluate your effectiveness using bucket five, the data bucket.

My data bucket used for keeping vital information at my fingertips is:

_____ Paper

_____ Electronic

_____ I'm not that organized

0	1	2	3	4	5	6	7	8	9	10

Not		Somewhat		Highly
Effective		Effective		Effective

Bucket Six — The Communication Bucket

There is one more bucket that all of us use. It's our electronic communications bucket or, in other words, our voicemail/email. Voicemail is not a major problem for most people, and most people don't abuse it.

Email, on the other hand, is a minefield of distractions, irrelevancies, and a great temptation for time-wasting. It is, however, the biggest part of our communication bucket, and an essential component of time management. We will address email later in the book when we discuss the skill of focusing. In the meantime, please evaluate your effectiveness with your communication bucket.

When evaluating my communication bucket used for oral and written communication:

_____ I control it

_____ It controls me

My effectiveness rating is:

0   1   2   3   4   5   6   7   8   9   10

Not   Somewhat   Highly
Effective   Effective   Effective

Based upon your style, pick paper or electronic tools you will really use. If you are a visual person, you may be most comfortable with paper. Don't let your peers intimidate you into going with an electronic tool if you know you won't use it. Here's a clue—if you use your

PDA only as an address/phone directory, you are probably better off using paper. On the other hand, if you prefer electronic tools and all of the bells and whistles they offer, they can be very useful. The key is in finding what works for you, and then making sure you've always got your six-pack handy:

- Bucket One—Your Monthly Calendar

- Bucket Two—Your Catch-All Bucket

- Bucket Three—Your Daily Bucket

- Bucket Four—Your Memory Bucket

- Bucket Five—Your Fingertip Data Bucket

- Bucket Six—Your Communication Bucket

Carry your time in six buckets. Check each bucket every day so that nothing falls through the cracks. It's easy once you pick and use your buckets. Ridiculously easy!

Chapter 4

ARRANGE YOUR PLATE
Think Inside the Box

The old way of thinking has been to place emphasis on the linear nature of time. Digital clocks blink away our life from the past to the present to the future. Often we find ourselves racing against time lines. It reminds us of the old saying, "The hurrier I go, the behinder I get."

What if we think of time as space? Time is the space in which we live. Just as a box is a space we fill with goods, an hour is a "time box" we fill with activities. Looking at time as space makes it easier to manage.

When we begin to look at an hour as a space in which we will execute activities, we are forced to be more realistic when we plan. A box—whether it's cardboard or time—can only hold so much.

We think most people intuitively recognize time as space. They refer to their day as a plate, which is limiting and they have too much on it. Furthermore, they don't seem to know what to do about it. Yet, each day a new miracle occurs—we are given a fresh plate consisting of twenty-four spaces of time called hours, into which we can pack any activities we choose.

We are so committed to treating time as space that we felt the need for a new bucket design—a design that would provide twenty-four "daily miracle time boxes" that followed the revolution of a board game, and would help us visualize time as space. (See **Figure 5** on pages 48 and 49.) You can download this design at our website www.attackyourday.com. We suggest you use the activity game for one week. When you get really good at it, you apply the technique to whatever tool you use, paper or electronic.

So, what activities are on your plate today? Did you take some time to arrange your plate? Or do you let others come along and throw their stuff on your plate? The *too-much-on-my-plate* challenge cannot be resolved without developing a simple and very enjoyable ritual. That ritual is to make a daily appointment with yourself to arrange your activities for the day. Call it planning if you like, but we prefer the term *arranging*.

I sometimes ask people if they plan their day. Often they will respond by saying, "Sure, here's my list." But, making a list isn't planning. Everyone is running around with lists. We agree with the British humorist who said, "The only important question in life is: what will I do next?"

Planning in advance will help you determine what you'll do next as you arrange the order for accomplishing the activities on your list. The challenge is that our most important resource—our time—is limited. As we mentioned above, each day we have twenty-four time spaces. Each of these time spaces of opportunity consists of one hour or sixty minutes.

THINK IN TERMS OF RESULTS

ATTACK YOUR DAY!

Figure 5 (Left Side)

The Activity Game

6AM	7AM	8AM	9AM
	Planning		Sales calls

5AM	Directions:
	1. Create your activity list below.
	2. Select a time box for each activity & schedule.
	3. Document activity notes to the right.
	Tip: Color your choices. red, green, yellow. (refer to book)

TODAY'S ACTIVITIES

4AM	✓
	Sales calls
	Client proposal
	Staff meeting
	Performance review
3AM	Customer complaint

2AM	Pick up milk!
	Exercise
	Pick up cleaning
	Jack's soccer game
	30 min of reading

1AM	12AM	11PM	10PM
			Reading

ARRANGE YOUR PLATE

Figure 5 (Right Side)

Think Inside the Box

10AM	11AM	12PM	1PM
	Proposals		

TODAY'S NOTES   03 / 22 / 11

Meeting - Report due Friday, review manual.

Pef Review - On track to meet goals. Need to increase product knowledge.

Complaint - Mr. Jones, product arrived damage. Send out new product, reference #HP2KRE10.

2PM — Staff meeting

3PM — Perf review

4PM

5PM — Cleaning

9PM	8PM	7PM	6PM
	Exercise	P/U milk	Soccer game

Here's the challenge: how do you arrange all of the activities on your plate so they will fit into your twenty-four hours? In addition, how do you make room in these time spaces for the expected/unexpected? How do you arrange the activities on your plate in a way that strikes a balance between self, family, work, and service responsibilities? And finally, as you execute activities around the clock, how do you manage your personal energy?

I think we would all agree the arranging challenge can be daunting. That's why so many people don't face it head on. However, investing no time in arranging your day leaves you more vulnerable to interruptions, distractions and general chaos.

You will be less vulnerable to interruptions and distractions if you are good at applying the third key skill of activity management: the ability to arrange activities; in other words, managing what's on your plate.

Most people face each new day with two big questions looming over them. The first question each day is this: "What's on my plate today?" The second question is, "How in the world will I get all of these activities done?" The solution lies in a concept we discussed earlier, that of making an appointment with yourself each day where you take time to arrange what's on your plate.

It's been our experience that most people only take one to five minutes each day to do this. It reminds me of an old expression my mother used when I was a young boy. After cleaning the house she would sometimes say, "I just gave it a lick and a promise." Have you ever heard that expression? Even as a young boy, I could figure out that it meant she hadn't taken much time, that she hadn't been very thorough, and that she didn't do it very well.

When people only give their planning time a "lick and a promise," they are usually frustrated, out of control, and their day controls them rather than the other way around.

There are so many issues to consider while arranging that it is impossible to do it in one or two minutes. Some of the things you need to consider are:

- Arranging creative activities during the time of day you are most creative.

- Arranging for availability with others when input is required.

- Arranging time to isolate yourself from others so you can focus on high priorities.

- Arranging time to manage your energy.

- Considering the schedules of family members and arranging time for them.

- Considering how you will arrange time to deal with the expected/unexpected. (This is an oxymoron that makes sense.)

When you stop to think about all of these things, it becomes very clear why time management is hard for most people instead of ridiculously easy. It's hard because people don't take the time to arrange their day.

Because You're Worth It

If you want time management to be easy, you need to "take-it-easy" for 30 minutes by yourself every day. Be a "lone arranger" and let your mind, your subconscious, and your heart guide you.

Let's discuss the process of arranging the day. It's not only an enjoyable experience, but it can increase your effectiveness exponentially. You'll also discover it can help you reduce stress. The resources you'll need to arrange your day are:

✓ A place to be alone

✓ Thirty minutes

✓ A best time

✓ Your time management tools

Let's begin with **resource number one**, a place where you can be alone to plan. This place needs to be away from any noise or distractions that apply to you. It also needs to be a place where you can sit, think, and write. These criteria eliminate your shower because, while a shower is a great place to think, it is a lousy place to write. The criteria also eliminate your car while you are driving, or riding with somebody else.

HOME AND/OR WORK

A final word about your special alone place is that you'll find it works best if you use it consistently as the place where you plan/arrange. Think of this as your *space-place*. It's great to have some space in a place you can be alone for a while.

Resource number two is 30 minutes each day reserved for arranging time. Why 30 minutes? A planning/arranging advantage seldom talked about is this important concept—when planning is not rushed, your subconscious mind and your heart have a chance to engage and assist you with the planning process.

Your subconscious mind will feed to you considerations you might otherwise overlook. It will give you a chance to evaluate with your heart the plans you've made for the day. When you do this—listen for intuitive promptings and follow them—it is likely that you will make better decisions.

Thirty minutes also benefits you in other ways. It gives you a chance to take a deep breath and reduce your stress. You will feel more in control, and you *will* be more in control.

Five Times the Outcome

Depending on the nature of your tasks, some will require more than 30 minutes to plan. Maybe that makes you even more nervous about setting aside sufficient time to plan. Consider this old axiom, "For every minute you plan/arrange, you get three times the execution." In our opinion, that's very conservative. We believe that for every minute we plan, we can actually get five times the execution. You can too.

3 TO
5 TIMES

There is nothing more crucial in activity management than taking 30 minutes each day for arranging the order for accomplishing activities. It pays huge dividends.

Sadly, for many, it never happens because of the big lie some people tell themselves. The one that goes like this: "I don't have time to plan/arrange today!" Isn't that the very reason they need to plan? Everybody has time to plan. If they don't plan/arrange, then "lack of planning" or "lack of arranging" becomes their plan. This is a negative, hazardous habit. It is hazardous to your health because, without a plan, stress is increased. It is hazardous to your work-life balance because, without careful planning and purposeful arranging, personal life and family life suffer. It is hazardous to your career because without planning/arranging you operate less efficiently than you could. All of these hazards make time management tough instead of ridiculously easy.

Don't cheat yourself. This is the fastest way to get attacked. Set aside sufficient time daily for you and attack your day. Yes, YOU. It is time for you to slow the pace; time for you to be isolated from chaos; time for you to activate a friend and partner called your subconscious and to engage your heart.

Resource number three is a best time for you to arrange your day. What do we mean by a best time? Some of us are morning people and others of us are night people. If you are a morning person, then set aside time in the morning to plan/arrange. If evening would be a better time for you to plan the upcoming day, then that's when you should do it.

Just remember, the best time to plan is connected to when your best place is available. As we've already mentioned, this place is a place of solitude, totally free of interruptions and distractions. At first, some people think such a place does not exist. With some creativity and a desire to find such a place, almost everyone can.

DAYTIMER
LAPTOP
CELLULAR

Resource number four is your time management tool(s) of choice. The specifics of those tools were discussed in Chapter two, where you were advised to use the tool or combinations of tools that serve you best. As a reminder, the resources you'll need to arrange your day are:

✓ A place to plan in solitude

✓ Thirty minutes reserved for planning/arranging time

✓ A best time of day for you to plan

✓ Your time management tools

You are now ready to arrange your day and it's as easy as one, two, three! Practice these three easy steps each day during your 30 minutes of alone time. If you do, you'll have the assurance nothing will fall through the cracks. Also, your ability to accomplish value-added activities should increase substantially.

Easy as One, Two, Three

Step One: Decide which activities to put on your plate for today. If you look at everything on your plate as though it has the same value, the day seems overwhelming and intimidating. On the other hand, if you look at what's on your plate through the metaphor of the traffic light, it is not as overwhelming. You see activities for what they are in terms of payoff: red, green, yellow, and gray.

But wait! How do you decide what to put on your plate in the first place? I'm talking about activities other than the ones that are tossed on your plate by others.

It's simple. During the 30 minutes you are spending on alone time in your space place, simply check each of the buckets. Then move the activities you'd like to accomplish today into today's bucket, bucket three. We suggest a routine in the following order:

1. Check bucket one, your monthly calendar. Move any scheduled commitments on your calendar for today into the appointments section of today's bucket three.

2. Next, look in bucket two, your catch-all bucket. At this point, aren't you pleased you have a catch-all bucket where you've centralized all the odds and ends you need to worry about rather than searching

for little pieces of paper and notes written on almost anything? Scan your catch-all bucket and you may see, for example, a reminder to buy a wedding gift for a friend. Move that activity into the daily bucket, "buy gift." Remember, a catch-all bucket isn't going to be much help unless you look into it every day and move activities into bucket three in a timely way. Isn't this easy?

3. Now take a peek at yesterday's bucket three. If there is any activity remaining there that was not completed, move it into today's bucket three. For example, if you didn't finish your expense report yesterday, put it on your activity list for today.

4. Then take a look at bucket four, the memory bucket, for yesterday. If you documented something that requires follow-up action, you can move it to today's activity list. Perhaps such an activity could be a commitment to fax an associate a report, or, if there is no rush, you can drop it in your catch-all bucket where it will not be forgotten.

5. Where do you go next? Check your information bucket, where you carry your planned future outcomes, your goals. Perhaps you have planned a summer vacation to Europe. Decide on an activity you could do today such as "order brochures." Doing that activity will

move you forward on your vacation activity path. Executing goal-related activities each day speeds you along toward the outcomes you desire.

6. Next, check your communication bucket, voicemail and email. It's my personal preference to check voicemail first. If there is a serious emergency, a red activity, it's more likely to come by voicemail rather than email. Let's assume there is a call from Jose Tepete. Add that to your activity list and delete it from your message center. Simple. The fact that it's on your action list reduces the likelihood you will forget to make the call.

Now to the minefield called email. Yes, it's a great innovation, but one that, unfortunately, is abused by many. More people are knocked off track by email than anything else. Email is like having 50 to 100 people lined up outside the door, not in any order, and you allow each one to poke his or her head in your office door and take some of your time to tell you something.

Many people allow others to intrude via email when they wouldn't stand for it if they were physically outside their door, yet the amount of time wasted is just the same. Here's the point—don't get side tracked by heavy email traffic while you are arranging your day.

ATTACK YOUR DAY!

Use the traffic light metaphor to speed through your email congestion. Pick out the red events/activities that will require your immediate attention and move those to the action list in bucket three. Set aside a time to come back later to answer and sort out the greens and yellows. Of course, develop a delete button trigger finger for the grays.

You can see what you've put on your plate in the form of a list of planned activities. The sources for these activities were:

Activity	**Source**
Appointments	Bucket one, the calendar
Buy gift	Bucket two, the catch-all bucket
Expense report	Bucket three, yesterday's daily bucket
Email report	Bucket four, yesterday's memory bucket
Order brochures	Bucket five, fingertip data bucket
Call Jose	Bucket six, the communication bucket

When you have a bucket to hold everything and everything is in its bucket, and you check each bucket daily, nothing falls through the cracks. Not only is this easy, think of the peace of mind you will have. This process allows you to be like Albert Einstein, who said, "I never try to remember anything. I just write it down and know where to find it."

Okay. You've checked each tracking bucket as sources for building a list of activities to put on your plate for the day. That means you've completed step one in arranging activities. Arranging your day truly is as easy as one, two, three. Let's consider step two.

Step Two: In step two, you place a value on each activity to facilitate better choice making. It's easy. Remember the traffic light and decide which activities are red, green or yellow. Simply put the letter of the corresponding color in front of each activity. For example, R = Red, G = Green, and Y = Yellow.

Coding activities by color/value is how you get a perspective of your activities at the start of each day. Sometimes the colors can change as the context of the work environment changes. I call this chameleon prioritization. A chameleon changes color with the environment.

For example, a green activity can change to red, or a yellow activity to green if some unexpected event suddenly shifts your priorities.

What's on your plate today?

If you are looking at your plate like this, so that every one of those black dots represents an activity you must perform, that's pretty intimidating. Most people look at their plate that way.

But you and I, we don't have that problem anymore. All we have to do is color our choices. So now we look at our plate in color, each activity activity becomes red, green, or yellow.

For Best Results

For best results, the activities on your list should be primarily green. This is so important that I want to really emphasize it, so I'll say it again. *For best results, the activities on our list should be primarily green.* Green activities keep you on the activity path to achieve your desired outcomes. Again, just remember to do what your mother always said, "Eat your greens." Remember, green means go there. Go with the green as much as possible.

Step Three: Now on to step three in arranging your day. What needs to be considered here is when, where, and how you plan to accomplish the activities. While it is true your day will probably not materialize the way you initially arrange it, it will provide you with a strategy to use for negotiating with changes as the day requires it.

There are five friendly planning/arranging guides that can assist you in arranging your day. Let me introduce them to you. They are:

- Necessity

- Reality

- Practicality

- Efficiency

- Spontaneity

Let's see how these key words help you as you consider what's on your plate.

Necessity: First ask, "What things are absolute necessities today?" Then, schedule the actual time you plan to do the necessities as an appointment with yourself. Do necessities as early in the day as possible.

Reality: Next ask, "Am I in touch with reality?" Remember. Things always take longer than you think. A lot longer. So allow at least 20 percent more time to accomplish the activities than you think it will take.

Also, decide what time of day, in which time box, you will accomplish each activity on your plate. Give each green activity a space of time. When you schedule the time you plan to do things, it will help keep you in touch with reality.

Practicality: Next ask, "What's the most practical way to do these activities?" Plan time away from the chaos of the day to do vital, value-added activities. Also, group similar projects together. For example, if you have a certain amount of corresponding to do, do it all at once. Studies show when people "batch" activities they are more effective.

Efficiency: Now ask, "What's the most efficient way to get these activities done?" Consider what things on your plate can be delegated and do it. Match activities that require the most mental and physical effort with the times of day your energy reserves are highest.

Spontaneity: Finally, ask yourself, "How much time should I reserve for the expected/unexpected?" Always expect the unexpected. Never fill your plate totally. Always save some time to handle the pop-ups.

As you listen to these five planning guides with your intuitive ears, you'll be amazed at how well your days begin to work for you.

ATTACK YOUR DAY!

Be consistent in setting aside some time alone each day to go through the foregoing steps. Day after day, week after week, and month after month, you'll get better and better at activity arranging.

Remember, the ridiculously easy one, two, three steps are:

Step 1: Decide what activities to put on your plate.

Step 2: Place a value, a color value, on each activity.

Step 3: Use the planning guides to help you decide when, where, and how to accomplish the activities.

Chapter 5

DON'T JUST EXECUTE FLEXICUTE!
Learn to Turn on a Dime

Now let's talk about the next skill in activity management, the skill of flexicuting. Here's where we're headed with this one. You've arranged the order for accomplishing the day's activities, and you begin to work your plan. You know, however (because you've done a reality check), that your day will not go exactly as you arranged it.

On a typical day, you can expect to get caught in the crossfire of interruptions, the unexpected will bubble up, and demands will fall out of the sky at inconvenient times. Flexicuting will be required.

Okay, so we invented the word flexicuting because we can't think of a better way to describe this skill. Events are so fluid in today's work environment that we have to change, adapt, and shift our focus all day long. Flexicuting involves the ability to:

- Be as willing to leave your activity list when priorities shift as you are to stick with it.

- Be able to turn on a dime in the middle of the day when an opportunity presents itself.

- Have the wisdom to modify your work style on the spot, and be willing to walk the path of another person's style to collaborate and get things done.

- Develop the habit of reserving some time every day to deal with the expected/unexpected.

- Be wired 24/7/365 without letting it be a source of frustration.

The Newest and Best Survival Skill

Would you like to become better at flexicuting? Here's how. Recognize it's a survival skill by changing your mindset and practice the foregoing flexicuting skills daily. It can actually be quite fun.

In the new time paradigm, flexicuting involves the skills of both multi-tasking activities and alternate-tasking activities. It also requires the wisdom to know when to use and when to avoid either of these approaches.

We'll talk about multi-tasking first. In our society, the term multi-tasking is overused. Even worse, the skill has been elevated to the pinnacle of desirable abilities and we often find ourselves abused—and sometimes abusing—in the execution of multi-tasking because there are some guidelines to multi-tasking that most people aren't aware of.

The best advice I can give people is to **BEWARE OF MULTI-TASKING!** Here's why. When you are executing multiple activities at the same time, none of these activities has your complete focus. If you must multi-task, it should be done only when you combine simple, mindless tasks such as opening your mail and watching the news.

Beware of multi-tasking while engaging with another person; for example, opening and reading your mail while carrying on a business conversation with somebody in your office. Not only is this disrespectful and a put-down of the other person, it's very easy to miss a point or to misinterpret the communication.

My personal rule of thumb is never, never, never multi-task while carrying on a conversation with another person.

Multi-tasking, when abused, leads to *time contamination*. An example of time contamination would be taking your child out for pizza so you can have some quality one-on-one time together, and then taking a cell phone call for fifteen minutes while your child stares into space. Time contamination is also working on your laptop while supposedly watching your child's soccer game.

Alternate-tasking is the natural result of being wired 24 hours a day, 7 days a week, and 365 days a year (24/7/365). Living under these conditions, it makes sense to alternate our work and personal life activities in a way that we can fully experience both. While multi-tasking can contaminate time, alternate-tasking does not.

Be Where You Are

Alternate-tasking is being 100 percent where you are. Be 100 percent in the pizza shop with your child and then place the call after the pizza outing. Alternate-tasking permits us to fully engage all activities without dilution or contamination of the experience.

Alternate-tasking can help you get more done in less time than multi-tasking because, when you are fully engaged, you are more efficient and productive.

Flexicuting also involves the oscillation of our daily activities. This too is part of the flexicuting skill. In other words, we alternate activities that require intense concentration of effort with activities that are easier and much less stressful. The easier activities give you a chance to recover your energy and then re-engage again.

Here's how I oscillate. I spend a lot of time working from my office at home. Typically, I'll schedule the activity of telephone coaching with a client, followed by thirty minutes of paper pushing. Then, I might do another period of coaching, followed by taking some time to get out of my office and run an errand. This is what we call making waves during the day. It's a way to manage our energy as well as our time. It can be a real downer to run out of energy before we run out of activity on our action list.

One of the foremost experts in the country on this subject is Dr. James Loehr, who co-wrote, among other books, *The Power of Full Engagement*. His advice is to manage our day as a series of sprints, each followed by adequate recovery time. If you are executing activities all day long as a marathon, it's likely you won't be as effective and will possibly burn yourself out by the end of the day.

Flexicuting and making waves during the day is not only ridiculously easy—it can be ridiculously fun as well.

Use Your Own Style

Flexicuting involves understanding both activity management styles, then using the one that works for you to get things done.

There are two styles for executing what's on our *time plate*. You probably know somebody who eats one type of food at a time. In other words they might first eat their chicken, then the potatoes and then the broccoli. They completely finish one type of food before proceeding to the next.

Some people clear their *time plate* the same way. They execute activities in linear order, starting with what they consider to be the highest priority to the lowest priority. Hence the classic method of prioritizing using the A, B, C, 1, 2, 3 methodology found in other time management programs. For a more efficient approach remember to prioritize using color: Red, Green, and Yellow. Red (R) represents activities that are *vital and urgent*, requiring attention first. Green (G) represents activities that are *vital/not urgent* and should be done second. Yellow (Y) represents activities that are *not vital/*

but have value, these should be done third. In other words, Yellow activities need to get done, but it's not vital they get done today. People that use this method are *singular activity managers*. They are effective and at the end of the day will have finished most of what is on their plates.

Others might take a bite of their dessert first. They alternate eating pieces of all portions on their plate moving from one to another. These are the *simultaneous activity managers*. Many are effective with this approach if they have good activity management skills, and at the end of the day they too will have finished most of what is on their plate.

In our society, simultaneous activity managers are often made to feel guilty because they operate with less structure. Don't feel guilty because you don't precisely follow the rules and laws of some time management gurus. We encourage people to use their own style, but understand both.

If you are simultaneous, you'll use your time management tools in a more relaxed way, probably won't write within the lines of your paper planners and you'll hate being a slave to electronic tools. That's okay. Whether you are a *singular* or *simultaneous* activity manger, it's not style that will determine your success or failure but whether or not you have the right activities on your plate in the first place. Work primarily in your own style, but remember a good flexicuter can use either style depending upon the circumstances.

Chapter 6

THE HOCUS POCUS
OF FOCUS
Make Time-Wasters Disappear

We've been talking about the four skills of activity management, which includes how to arrange the activities in your day. Activity arranging involves deciding what activities to put on your plate and giving those activities value. It is those value-added activities we should focus on to achieve high productivity. The fifth skill of activity management is the ability to focus.

You First

We talked in chapter two about learning to say no, or what we call strengthening our "no muscle." Interestingly, the first person we need to get good at saying no to is ourself. We are often our own worst enemy. We often break our focus for what are merely time-wasting activities. We identified time-wasters earlier as gray activities.

Developing the ability to say no to unnecessary interruptions and distraction activities is critical to being productive. Notice we said unnecessary. The last thing you would ever want to do is get rid of all of your interrupting activities. Some interruptions are essential, job-related, and necessary. We need to eliminate the ones that aren't necessary—the ones that are the true time-wasters.

The inability to say no to interruptions and distractions breaks our focus. To stay focused, all you need is the skill and will to say no and mean it.

Start learning to focus by taking a personal inventory of the negative activities that cause you to break your focus. Look carefully over the following list of self-imposed, internally-motivated focus breakers, and put a checkmark by the ones you do that break your ability to stay focused.

Self-Imposed, Internally Motivated, Focus Breakers*

_____ Insufficient planning

_____ Socializing

_____ Surfing the net

_____ Attempting to do too much

_____ Getting lost in details

THE HOCUS POCUS OF FOCUS

_____ Preoccupation

_____ Ineffective delegation

_____ Unwillingness to say "no"

_____ Arguing

_____ Lack of self-discipline

_____ Procrastination

_____ Failure to prioritize

_____ Your own errors

_____ Failure to listen carefully

_____ Your need to over-control

_____ Unrealistic time estimates

_____ Poorly defined goals

_____ Misplacing or losing items

_____ Failure to anticipate events or changes

_____ Responding to counterfeit urgency

*Source: Charles R. Hobbs, _Time Power_, Harper and Row.

Now that you've taken the survey, how did you do? Did you check a lot of focus breaker activities? If so, we have good news for you! All focus breaker activities that are self-imposed are 100 percent controllable. Be like a magician. Use some hocus pocus, and make them all disappear. The first step is using your "no muscle" on yourself.

Here's how you do that. Pick one focus breaker on the list that troubles you the most: for example, attempting too much. Attempting too much breaks our focus because we spread ourselves too thin. In your time management tool, write the positive version of your focus breaker to make it a focus maker. Instead of attempting too much, your goal is to be realistic about how much you attempt, so you could write, "I never attempt too much." Or, because some people prefer to always state things positively, you could write, "I am realistic about my daily goals."

Write this statement on your activity list every day. Practice it every day for the next three weeks. Practice it just as you would practice your golf swing, playing the piano, or anything you want to get better at. At the end of three weeks, it will be part of your work style to avoid attempting too much.

Next, pick another focus breaker on the list and control that one. Do this on an ongoing basis and your ability to focus will get better and better.

Don't try to control all of your focus breakers at once. Work on one at a time throughout the year. As you do, your "no muscle" will get stronger and stronger. It's not all that hard, and in the end it is highly rewarding.

Now, what about all the focus breaker activities that are system-imposed or externally motivated? These are the activities we are often sucked into that cause us to break our focus as well as make us feel irritated and frustrated. Can we say no to all of those? Not really, but to many of them we can. First, complete the following assessment. Check the System-imposed, Externally Motivated Focus Breakers you encounter most often.

System-imposed, External Focus Breakers*

_____ Meetings

_____ Delayed work

_____ Delayed decisions

_____ Inappropriate use of email, voicemail, etc.

_____ Computer problems (related to support)

ATTACK YOUR DAY!

_____ Poor communication

_____ Errors by others

_____ Telephone calls

_____ Frequent visits (drop-ins)

_____ Lengthy visits

_____ Poor definition of tasks or problems

_____ Unclear lines of authority

_____ Understaffing

_____ Lack of feedback

_____ Unclear roles

_____ Ongoing incompetence

_____ Conflicting priorities

_____ Emotional conflicts

_____ Changing instructions, priorities

*Source: Charles R. Hobbs, *Time Power*, Harper and Row.

What did you learn from that survey? Are you letting a lot of system-imposed challenges destroy your ability to focus? The way you address this type of focus breaker is to pick one interruption, distraction, or irritation that breaks your focus. Then ask yourself, "Is it within my power to do something about this?" If not, change your mindset, adapt, suck it up, and stop worrying about it! If you can do something about it, develop a plan and resolve it. Fix one focus breaker at a time, but work on a series of them throughout the year. That's the easy and most effective way.

Be Strong

The most common activities that break our focus are interruptions and distractions by others. If we have a wimpy "no muscle" then we will be dominated by them. Dealing with them is easy. All you really need to know are the four response options and the three focus techniques for saying no.

The four response options to interruptions are easy to use. How do you decide which one to choose? Simply color your choices as we described in the first chapter. The four response options are:

1. Respond and do it now when it's red.

2. Reschedule for a later time when it's green or yellow and can be postponed.

3. Refer it to someone else if it's not in your domain.

4. Refuse to do it when it's gray. This is when you use your "no muscle."

The four techniques for refusing or saying no are:

1. The Immediate Response Method

This is when you refuse a request on the spot, immediately after it is made. There are four elements you can include in your refusal statement to soften the response. The elements express:

- A desire to be helpful

- A singular reason you can't

- An expression of regret

- And a thank you for asking

Here's an example of the refusal statement using those elements. "I'd love to help but right now I just have too much on my plate, I'm really sorry but thank you for asking." This is a classy approach most people will feel good about.

Caution: When giving a singular reason for saying no such as your plate is full, don't give details. The more specific reasons you give, the less persuasive you'll sound. You are not obligated to give reasons.

2. The Delay Tactic

This is when you are unsure and you want to think through the request. People often say yes when they should say no because they are under the pressure of the moment. For example, use a simple statement such as, "I'd like to but I'm not sure I can. Give me some time to think about it and I'll get back to you." If, after thinking about it, you decide you can't, then use a refusal statement with the elements described above.

3. The Helping Hand Approach

This technique is driven by a sincere desire to be helpful even though you must say no. For example, recommend to the person somebody else who might assist them, or you could suggest alternative solutions. You might also agree to commit some limited time to it. It's good time management to always lend a helping hand when we can.

4. Just say NO

This takes courage. But when a person approaches you with "gray matter" just say NO. Remember, gray stands for activities that are a complete waste of time, such as office gossip. In our seminars we go through an exercise where participants stand up and yell in their loudest voice, "NO...NO, NO, NO. What part of no don't you understand! Can't you see that I am working here!"

Practice these techniques and your "no muscle" will get stronger and stronger.

Improving Your Life Quality

You've probably already noticed that the activity management skills we've been discussing throughout the book are all designed to do one thing. They are intended to improve your ability to focus upon and execute your most crucial work-life activities.

Activity _Choosing_ involves selecting the most important activities on which you should focus.

Activity _Tracking_ involves the skillful use of time management tools to ensure nothing falls through the cracks.

Activity _Arranging_ involves planning how, when, and where, and the order for focusing upon and executing the day's most vital activities.

Activity _Flexicuting_ involves the skill of shifting your focus throughout the day as priorities change.

Get What You Want

You probably also noticed that the first four skills all support the fifth activity management skill, which is focus.

In fact, everything we do in time management is designed to help us identify, focus upon, and accomplish our most vital work-life activities. Get what you want in life by managing your activities with these five skills. You can do it. It is easier than most people think. You can get better and better at it with daily and weekly practice.

The remainder of the book offers 101 productivity strategies to help you focus more effectively. Many are inspired and in some cases, have been taken directly from the Charles Hobbs Time Power Seminar and are used by permission. The rights to Time Power are currently owned by Day-Timer, Inc. and marketed by Trapper Woods International and affiliated partners.

We invite you to implement one productivity strategy each day. It takes just a minute or two to read and the investment of time can pay huge dividends throughout the day.

ATTACK YOUR DAY!

We also invite you to practice the five activity management skills on a daily basis, without exception. If you do, you'll find your skills will get better and better. Then, one day in the not-so-distant future, you might just say to yourself. "This really is ridiculously easy!"

Start today. Plan your attack, and then attack your plan. Best wishes for a rich and abundant life!

101

Productivity
Strategies

#1

LEVERAGE YOUR MIND! USE IT FOR THINKING, NOT REMEMBERING

Problem! There is not only more to do these days but more to remember. When your mind is cluttered with things you are trying to remember, it's not as free to focus on vital work activities.

Solution! Pick a time management tool that works best for you (either paper or electronic). Then, be meticulous about entering all appointments, dates, deadlines, and important information. Always carry it with you, and let the tool do your remembering for you. Freeing your mind this way should help you increase your focus and reduce stress.

#2

HOW TO DEAL WITH OVERWHELM, BEGIN WITH A SHIFT IN MIND-SET

Most people who are *consistently* overwhelmed are often attempting to do too much. They do not delegate. They allow too many interruptions. They are into their ego thinking they are the most capable solution to every problem. People who are overwhelmed frequently procrastinate themselves into crisis mode and are not good at life management.

These characteristics have in common a sense of self-importance. Make the appropriate adjustments on those characteristics that may apply to you—delegate, reschedule, say not yet, plan ahead and act! Then you'll be on your way to controlling the feeling of overwhelm.

Source: William A. Guillory

DO YOU WANT TO AVOID TIME CRUNCHES? GO FASTERTHAN TIME

We can't make time speed up and we can't make time slow down. We can, however, go faster than time. Go faster than time by deciding what events you want to occur on future dates. You can do that by describing them as written objectives—long-range goals. Then, plan/ arrange and execute the actions—intermediate goals— that will make your planned future events materialize. In this way you can get out in front of time.

People who are in control of their lives maximize this advantage. People who are out of control don't. They always find themselves in a time crunch. They let time overtake them by starting the above process too late. It's called procrastination.

#4

YOU CAN HAVE THE BEST OF BOTH PLANNING TIMES

Some will agree the best time to plan your day is early in the morning. This way, your mind has had a chance to incubate ideas during the night. You'll also be more refreshed.

Others say the best time to plan is the night before because you're under less pressure. Then, when you arise, you'll be able to hit the street running.

One of our clients uses a different approach, and for him it is very effective. He said "I split my planning time. I spend fifteen minutes creating an initial plan the night before, and then I validate it with fifteen more minutes of planning in the morning." That way, he capitalizes on the benefits of both morning and evening planning.

#5

HAVING A HARD TIME ENDING AN OVERLONG CALL OR VISIT?

Interrupt yourself! Try this. First, gain control of the conversation. Then in the middle of a sentence, abruptly stop talking, glance at your watch, and mention the time in an urgent manner. For example: "Oh! It's three-fifty! I need to get going." That's all it takes.

Notice the technique. It's honest and not threatening because it's never rude to interrupt yourself. Plus, it puts you in control. It breaks the conversation politely so you can be on your way.

WANT TO ACCELERATE YOUR PERSONAL PRODUCTIVITY?

Use blank spaces of time well. A blank space of time is any amount of time in which you are waiting for others, or you are put on hold for whatever reason. Perhaps you are waiting for a meeting to start.

Blank spaces can be used in two general ways. One: use blank spaces of time to complete mini-tasks that might take only a few minutes. Always have something with you that you could be working on, or carry an article with you to read. Two: use blank spaces to manage your energy level. It often takes only five minutes or so to win back energy. Change a routine; take a walk around the building, do stretching or some deep breathing. These techniques can work wonders. It's just as important to manage your energy as it is to manage your time.

Blank spaces of time are golden opportunities. Don't let them go to waste.

#7

NOT ENOUGH TIME FOR YOU? PAY YOURSELF FIRST

On airplanes, in case of an emergency, we are told to put on our own oxygen masks first and then to help our child. When investing money, we are encouraged to pay ourselves first. Why? We have to take care of ourselves to serve effectively. But a mind-set that says we must first satisfy the demands of others often leaves us lacking energy for the things we care about. This ultimately leaves us with less energy and resources, not only for ourselves, but for others as well.

Try this: plan 30 minutes for yourself every day. Make an appointment with yourself! Note in your Day-Timer® Organizer not only the time, but also the place. Honor the commitment.

#8

TRY COUNTER-POINT TIME MANAGEMENT?

Do you get stressed waiting in lines? Or, maybe traffic congestion is driving you crazy. Try counter-point time management. It's simple! Plan to grocery shop, run errands, go to lunch, or commute at times different than the masses. It will save you time. One executive found that leaving fifteen minutes earlier for work saved him thirty minutes on the other end.

BUILD A "RESULTS LIST" – NOT A "TO-DO LIST"

I've never liked the term "to-do list." A to-do list connotes procrastination because it's only a list of intentions.

To be effective, build a "results list" at the beginning of each day and label it Results List! This is a list of things you will make happen with the investment of your time and energy. Make the listed results absolutely specific. For example: "call twenty clients" not "call clients."

At the end of the day, you'll have measurable results for your effort. You will also feel a sense of self-management power because you were effective. Power is the ability to produce effect. Power is the ability to get results. Make each day a powerful day with a results list.

#10

TWO QUESTIONS THAT CAN HELP YOU SAVE TIME

It's often said that the biggest waste of time is doing something well that needn't be done at all. It might feel good to get it done, but why do it if it isn't necessary? Analyze your actions with two questions:

1) What am I doing now that doesn't need to be done by me or anyone else?

2) What am I doing that others can do? When you have the answers, you can lighten your load.

Source: Charles R. Hobbs – Time Power

#11

THANK GOODNESS FOR INTERRUPTIONS

If you have interruptions, you probably have a job and that's good. The last thing you would ever want to do is get rid of interruptions coming to you as part of your job. These are *necessary* interruptions.

The real problem with interruptions is when they are unnecessary. These are the true time robbers, and they can and should be controlled. Separate necessary and unnecessary interruptions by asking yourself the filter question: "Is what's happening right now necessary for the existence, continuation, and well-being of the organization?" If the answer is no, then say, "No" to the interruption and refocus on the task at hand. The ability to say no in a non-threatening way in appropriate situations is an instant time saver. It gets easier and easier with practice.

#12

WHY NOT MEET IN THE OTHER PERSON'S OFFICE?

When having a one-on-one meeting with somebody it is often a good idea to meet in their office. There are several reasons for this. First, it's a cordial, nice thing to do. Also, they get your undivided attention because you won't be subject to the normal interruptions and distractions of your own office space. Perhaps just as important is the idea that when it's time to end the meeting, you'll be more in control. It's easier to politely leave someone else's office than it is to ask them to leave yours. And there's another bonus! Going to someone else's space gives you a chance to move around, stretch, and win back some energy.

Source: Time Power Seminar

#13

FACING A DIFFICULT WORK-LIFE CHOICE? ASK YOURSELF THE CHRYSTAL BALL QUESTION

In the process of developing a career, we make crucial work-life decisions—sometimes without conscious awareness of their long-term consequences.

Taking responsibility for your work-life choices begins with deciding what's most important to you in both the short-term and long-term, and learning to reconcile the two. It means making choices based upon projecting the consequences of those decisions into a "probable future."

The crystal ball questions are: "Is that future, with its probable consequences, acceptable to me and my family?" or, "What impact will this decision have on my life five years from now? Ten years from now?"

ARE YOU GUILTY OF GUILT?

There's a work-life integration stumbling block for some people. It is known as "SIGS", or Self-Imposed Guilt Syndrome. Guilt is a natural result of attempting to split our lives between work and personal. Many feel guilty at work for not being home, and guilty at home for not being at work.

It is important to realize that very often this guilt is self-imposed, and that it is nearly always counter-productive to work-life quality and balance. Two things are helpful in overriding "SIGS." First, practice *work-life integration* instead of work-life separation. See yourself as one holistic person, not two separate people. Second, transform your thinking by controlling and eliminating guilty thoughts. It's silly to keep sticking pins in yourself.

#15

ACTIVITIES RULE, NOT THE CLOCK!

An activity is something we do. An activity is the basic unit of our life's design. Results are determined by the activities we choose and how we arrange to get them done.

How well do you choose and arrange your daily activities? In business, select activities that are essential for the existence, continuation, and the well-being of your organization or your family. Avoid trivial activities.

Here are four activity selection questions you can apply on a daily basis:

1. Is this activity a step toward the achievement of a goal?

2. Is this activity a good time investment?

3. If I don't do the activity, who will it affect? Will anyone suffer?

4. Is the activity necessary for the existence, continuation or well-being of the organization? My family?

Knowing what to choose and what to refuse is what it's about.

Activities rule, not the clock. The clock is nothing more than a measurement tool. Learn to be a good activity chooser!

#16

RATIONALIZATION – IT CAN PUT A CHOKE-HOLD ON PRODUCTIVITY

Rationalization is an attempt to justify inappropriate action or inaction. Sometimes people see it as a friend because it can help protect self-esteem. However, it is not a friend when it is used to avoid doing a vital task we don't want to do.

Perhaps you are avoiding a call to an unhappy customer. You know the customer or client will be angry and you rationalize by saying something like, "This probably isn't a good time." Of course, you know it is an excuse.

A close look at rationalization reveals its first-cousin relationship to procrastination. Why? Because rationalization is used to justify putting things off.

Here is the good news! Rationalization is a self-imposed time-waster. This means you can control it. Listen to your self-talk and recognize when you are doing it. Replace those thoughts with a "can do" and "will do" attitude.

ARE YOU GETTING CAUGHT IN TIME TRAPS?

It is easy to overlook certain time traps. They are patterns of using time that provide no positive return.

To become aware of time traps, take a careful look at your habitual patterns. These might include such things as watching the same news over and over again on cable T.V., or attending endless meetings not requiring your input. Other habitual patterns could include getting side-tracked by junk email, performing needless tasks, drifting into preoccupation, or even encouraging needless interruptions.

Start with self-observation. Then set goals that establish different patterns. Watching for time traps and establishing different patterns can help you refocus several hours of time per day on more productive activities.

#18

WANT AN IDEA THAT CAN GIVE YOU A QUANTUM JUMP IN PRODUCTIVITY?

Rationalization and procrastination are two personal habits that become barriers to getting things done. The truth is… habits are hard to break. But, the good news is… they are easy to replace. You can replace these two personal habits with more productive ones.

Here's a good replacement. Try this personal goal that can be repeated over and over again as an affirmation: "I will always do the thing that needs to be done, when it needs to be done, in the way it needs to be done, whether I like it or not!"

Begin right now. Go back to the previous paragraph and say that affirmation out loud. Choose to repeat it several times a day as an affirmation. Write it in your planner each day as a high-priority goal. Practice it until it becomes a habit. Watch your productivity and self-esteem soar to new heights.

Source: Time Power Seminar

BEING ON TIME FOR APPOINTMENTS IS MORE THAN GRACIOUS!

We all face situations from time to time that can cause us to be late for meetings and appointments. Chronic tardiness, however, can diminish our professional reputation. It also irritates others. How is your track record?

One reason people are often late is that they fail to manage transition time. Transition time is the time required to move from one activity to the next and/or from one location to the next, whether it's just down the hall or across town.

Here's an idea to improve punctuality: Write in your planner not just when the meeting starts, but also when you are going to leave to go to the meeting. Allow a little extra buffer time too because we are often stopped by a co-worker in a hallway, and there is always the possibility of a traffic jam.

Punctuality communicates to others: "I'm a professional and you are important to me." Tardiness sends another message.

Make it appoint to always be early to appointments and make it fun. Schedule appointments at off times like 9:58 am, or 12:22 pm and my favorite is 5:55 pm.

#20

AVOID THE RICOCHET EFFECT AND STAY ON TASK

The ricochet effect is the human tendency to lose focus after an interruption. Interruptions break our continuity of thought. They can result in our failure to refocus on what we were doing prior to the distraction. This can minimize our effectiveness.

Making a prioritized list at the beginning of the day is a good way to correct this tendency, but only if we keep the list visible at all times. When the list is constantly in our view, it serves as a tool to re-anchor our attention after an interruption. Sailing through the day without something to remind us to keep on task is like trying to navigate without a rudder.

#21

KNOW SOMEBODY WHO "SPINS THEIR WHEELS" AT WORK?

They are on the slippery slope of indecisiveness. Indecisiveness is the enemy of getting started. Similar to a car in neutral, which can't go anywhere until it's in gear, indecisiveness puts you in neutral-time.

What's the best way to stop "spinning wheels" and "get in gear?" First, take the time to create clarity of purpose. Set specific goals that can be broken down into daily actions. Then, prioritize the actions. Clarity is the mother of decisiveness.

MONEY! NOT THE ONLY COST OF CONSUMPTION

When you buy a boat or a summer home, or any number of material possessions, you always know what it will cost in dollars.

How often do you stop to consider the cost of TIME? Most material possessions require some sort of maintenance time. *Using* possessions requires time too. Some people reach a point where much of their time is controlled by what they *have* (stuff) in contrast to what they *need*. If this is you, consider getting rid of "stuff" that needlessly consumes time. You'll end up with the luxury of more freedom of choice.

#23

INTER-PERSONAL CONFLICT – A PRODUCTIVITY TIME BOMB!

Ever notice how a two- or three-minute conflict with another person can drain more energy from your system than a full day's work? If you carry that emotional upset with you and then take it home day after day, you make it grow. Down goes your own productivity, and down goes the productivity of those to whom you complain.

Persistent, unresolved conflict is a time-waster of the worst kind. Have the courage to fix it fast. If necessary, seek help from a human resource person. You will conserve both time and energy.

#24

DO YOU RUN OUT OF ENERGY BEFORE YOU RUN OUT OF ITEMS ON YOUR ACTION LIST?

Your two most vital resources are energy and time. Both must be simultaneously managed. Take short breaks governed by your body clock, not the clock on the wall. Eat lunch for sure, but make it light, not heavy. Schedule your most difficult tasks when your energy cycles tend to be the highest. Plan to do easier tasks during your more difficult energy cycles. Finally, get plenty of sleep.

Taking time to manage your energy is like running on personal "100%" octane fuel.

#25

ARE THINGS FALLING THROUGH THE CRACKS?

A bucket is used for collecting and carrying things. Personal time management tools are actually buckets where you collect, carry, and track information. Whether you use a paper tool or an electronic tool, make sure you have six buckets.

- Bucket One: The *monthly calendar*. Use it for carrying future events that are scheduled.

- Bucket Two: The *catch-all* bucket. Use it to collect and carry activities (things to do) that are not yet scheduled.

- Bucket Three: The *daily* bucket. Use it to plan and track today's activities such as today's schedule and action list.

- Bucket Four: The *memory* bucket. This is the place to record information that needs to be saved for future reference.

- Bucket Five: The *fingertip data* bucket. The place to carry necessary data, including goals, projects, and vital information (addresses and phone numbers) so it can be quickly accessed.

- Bucket Six: The *communication* bucket. This is your voicemail and email bucket where you receive and hold incoming messages.

Very little will fall through the cracks if you check each bucket daily, and move events and activities from one bucket to another when appropriate.

#26

AVOID TIME DEBT!

Like financial debt, too much *time-debt* can be a heavy burden to bear. You get yourself into *time-debt* by saying "yes" to too many future commitments. In actuality, saying "yes" to a future commitment is a verbal promissory note. Promising away your future creates stress. You know at some point those time commitments to other people will come due. Can you keep your promises? Do you really want to? It all hangs over your head.

Make it a point to be as frugal with your time as you are with your money. Respond to requests for your time honestly. If you know you don't intend to or just plain can't keep the time-promise, then graciously decline the commitment. Maybe you don't know if you'll have time. Be honest about that too. Say something like, "I'd like to help you with that, but right at this moment I'm just not sure how my schedule will play out with some projects I already have going. Can I get back with you?" In this way you've offered to consider the request based on your own personal time needs.

Be generous with your time, yes, but avoid the needless stress of *time-debt*.

#27

PRACTICE PLANNED SPONTANEITY

Planned spontaneity is an oxymoron but it works. Here's the idea! Spontaneity enriches any activity that would otherwise be more mundane. For example, try this. Open your Day-Timer® Organizer at random and put a red dot on a future page. Then close it and forget about it. When the day finally arrives on which you've placed the red dot, do something unexpected for somebody. For example, send some flowers for no reason at all. You'll find the activity is far more joyous and impactful than when the flowers are expected.

Source: Gary Rifkin

#28

WHAT IS BETTER THAN THE BEST MEMORY?

There's an old Chinese proverb that says, "The palest ink is better than the best memory." In today's environment, making written notes is crucial! Making only mental notes is risky!

Information comes at us relentlessly from telephone calls, drop-in visitors, voicemail, email, text messages and handwritten notes from others. Some of the information needs recording for future reference.

For absolute control, make your notes in a formal daily journal with each page dated. Keep it with you. This way, you'll always have a permanent place to write. It's more professional and less risky than grabbing any old piece of paper within your reach. File your journals in sequence. Years later, you'll always be able to find crucial information.

#29

CONTROLLING INTERRUPTIONS BEGINS BEFORE THEY OCCUR

Many people complain about too many interruptions in a day. Few have an advance strategy for minimizing interruptions.

The key to minimizing unwanted interruptions is to look at your day and plan your strategy in advance. A plan reduces your vulnerability.

Plan high-priority time away from your normal environment so you're not around to receive the interruption. Schedule interruptions by letting people know the times of day you'll be available. Screen calls and visitors. As you become consistent with these techniques, co-workers get used to your style and you have fewer interruptions.

#30

IN TODAY'S ENVIRONMENT, SAYING NO IS AN INSTANT TIME-SAVER

Saying no is everyone's prerogative. Here are four simple tips from author Jo Coudert that help you do it in a way that's not harsh or unkind.

1. "I'm glad you asked, but my schedule won't permit me to accept your offer."

2. "Let me think about it." (You seldom have to accept on the spot.)

3. Use humor. "I suppose you think I say no just because I'm mean! Well, it's true!"

4. "Sorry, but that's not something I do." (That's inarguable.)

Be ready. Say no when you mean it. In the long run, it's much easier than saying yes.

CAN YOU FLEXICUTE?

Okay, so we invented a word, but I can't think of a better way to describe this skill. Events are so fluid in today's work environment that we have to change, adapt and shift our focus all day long. Flexicuting involves the ability to:

- Be as willing to leave your action list when priorities shift as you are to stick with it.

- Be able to turn on a dime in the middle of the day when an opportunity presents itself.

- Have the wisdom to modify your work style on the spot, and be willing to walk the path of another person's style to collaborate and get things done.

- Be wired 24/7/365 without letting it be a source of frustration.

Would you like to become better at flexicuting? Here's how! Recognize it as a survival skill by changing your mind-set and practicing the foregoing skills daily. It's actually quite fun!

#32

EMAIL JAIL! THE DIRTY LITTLE SECRET

Email, like the telephone, is a business tool that facilitates communication. Also, like the telephone, it can be abused and often becomes a time-waster. This occurs when this wonderful technology is used for excessive "chit-chat" on company time. The covert nature of email permits us to do this while appearing to be engaged in work. It's easy to sit in a cubicle and visit with the outside world all day long. When this becomes a habit, we've put ourselves in email jail.

How do we bail ourselves out? Maintain a formal professional stance when using both telephone and email. Don't interrupt yourself all day long to check for messages. Remember to chat on your own time. Avoiding email jail will help you improve performance, feel better about yourself, and be respected as a professional.

#33

REDUCE OVERLONG TELEPHONE CALLS 30% - 50%

According to one long-distance carrier, the average unplanned telephone call lasts an average of ten minutes. A planned phone call lasts only seven minutes. So how long does a "carefully" planned phone call last? I believe telephone time can actually be cut in half when the call is carefully planned. Here's how:

Before dialing:

- Clarify the purpose of the call

- Create a simple agenda

- Establish a stop time

Then, make the call and stick with it. You save money. You save your time, and you save the other person's time too! They will appreciate it and be impressed with your professionalism.

#34

HOW OFTEN DO YOU MAKE APPOINTMENTS WITH YOURSELF?

You make appointments with others, but what about appointments with yourself? Check your appointment schedule for the past month. Did you make any "self" appointments and honor them like any other business commitment? Just hoping time will materialize for you to do your own stuff in between appointments with others is an ineffective alternative.

Making an appointment with yourself to accomplish a high-priority task is exceptionally productive. Why not make appointments with yourself every day? Simply identify the task, set the time, screen interruptions and get the job done in a meeting with you.

USE A TALK FILE TO AVOID INTERRUPTING OTHERS

One of the best time management tips I ever learned was the use of a "talk file." If you communicate with a number of people on an on-going basis, you could label an index tab in your planning tool "talk file." Then put a sheet of paper in that section for each person with whom you communicate.

As you are working during the day, thoughts will come to mind about issues you need to discuss with individuals in your file. Rather than call and interrupt those people on the spur of the moment (which is the natural inclination), jot the thought down under their name in your talk file. Begin to build a digest of issues for each person. This way, you will reduce the number of times you interrupt others; and, when you do talk, you won't forget a thing! In addition, your peers will appreciate you even more.

#36

HAVE YOU BECOME THE GO-TO GURU?

People who unwittingly set themselves up to be the go-to guru in an office usually have three characteristics. They are exceptionally knowledgeable, extremely nice and seldom say no. Once such a person is discovered, everyone gravitates there to save time. After all, it's easier to ask the go-to guru than find answers themselves.

If you are the person everyone seeks for help, you'll reach a point where it's not fair to you! Consequently, you won't have enough time to do your own work. If this is you, then set some parameters and limits. Direct others where to go rather than give them all the answers. People will soon get the point, and you'll have fewer interruptions and distractions. The inability to say no when it's appropriate is the first cousin to overwhelm.

TRY PAPER PRIORITY PILING TO CLEAR THAT CLUTTERED DESK

Like to dig your desk out from underneath piles of paper? Set aside an hour where you can work free of interruptions. Go through each paper, one at a time, and sort them into three stacks. Create a red stack for papers that are vital and need immediate attention. Build a green stack for papers that are important, and a yellow stack for papers of limited value. Of course, some papers will get tossed right into the recycle bin.

Leave the red stack on your desk. Put the green and yellow papers out of sight for a few days. You might discover later that some of those things needn't be done at all.

WHEN IS DROPPING SOMETHING A GOOD THING?

If you feel as though you don't have sufficient time to accomplish everything, look around for an unnecessary activity or two you can drop.

An activity is something we do. Anything we do requires time. Most people habitually do activities that aren't necessary and don't have much value. Find something you can stop doing and replace it with a more positive activity, such as personal reading time. You will have discovered a treasure.

Right now, stop and decide what you can stop doing!

#39

USE THE DIRECT APPROACH TO SAVE YOUR TIME

For years, time management experts have suggested non-verbal communication techniques to end overlong phone calls and office visits. With some people they work; with others, they don't.

The direct approach always works. When somebody engages you, call their attention to your schedule, and set a front time limit. When the agreed-upon time has expired, it's easier to end the visit. How simple is this? But very infrequently done!

#40

PROCRASTINATING ON A PROJECT? USE THE COLD SWIMMING POOL TECHNIQUE

What's the best way to get into a cold swimming pool? Scream and jump right in. If you want to hammer out that project you don't like, treat it like a cold swimming pool.

The first step is to arrange everything the night before. Clear your desk and lay out all the necessary items you will need to complete the project. Make it clear that no one is to distract you in the morning.

The next morning, go to work an hour earlier than normal. Don't go through your normal routines. Take that cold plunge first thing in the morning, and just jump right into the project. It's likely that you'll be pleased and amazed with the results. How about a cold swim tomorrow morning?

#41

TRAP PAPER BEFORE IT TRAPS YOU

One thing is guaranteed. The onslaught of paper will persist even in an electronic environment. If we don't process it routinely and systematically, it can swamp us.

Routinely means you process it periodically to limit it from building up. *Systematically* means attempting to handle it once using the TRAP formula, which is based on a system created by author Stephanie Winston in *The Organized Executive.*

There are basically four things you can do with a piece of paper as it comes across your desk:

T – Toss it   A – Act on it

R – Refer it   P – Permanently file it

There is no time like the present to begin TRAP-ing your paper.

#42

INTEGRATE, DON'T CONTAMINATE, WORK-LIFE ACTIVITIES

Work-life integration is the alternate execution of work and personal life activities in a manner that permits us to fully experience the quality of both.

Work-life contamination is the simultaneous execution of work and personal life activities in a manner that prevents us from fully experiencing the quality of either. This is commonly referred to as multi-tasking.

An example is: opening your mail while carrying on an important business conversation with somebody in your office. Not only is it impolite, you might miss something very important.

Resolve to integrate, not contaminate! Your life will be richer and fuller.

DON'T FORGET THE OTHER CLOCK!

The other clock I'm referring to is your body clock. That involves the bio-rhythms that occur during the twenty-four-hour day. This pattern includes the time when you are the most alert, have the best physical concentration, and when your energy ebbs and flows.

When planning your day, match activities to your bio-rhythms. For example, I'm the most creative and alert between 9:00 and 11:00 a.m. This is when I write. I sink into an energy trough between 2:00 and 3:00 in the afternoon—the best time for me to be on my feet supervising.

Start today to get in touch with your bio-rhythms, matching tasks accordingly. You'll get more done and enjoy your day more.

#44

A VALUABLE TIP
FROM A FRIEND

One of my long-time friends, who has been very successful, taught me the "Richards Principle," named for his father who practiced it throughout his life.

On numerous occasions over the years, as we faced business and life challenges, he quoted the principle to me. It goes like this: Plan, Simplify, and Be Strong!

The principle is good advice for anybody who wants a higher quality of life. Evaluate yourself on how effective you are at planning and simplifying your life. Make the necessary changes and then be strong at sticking with your plan. After all, it's your life to control and enjoy.

#45

THE POWER OF PROXIMITY

Proximity will work for you or against you. It all depends on you. We tend to focus on what's visible and readily accessible.

New Year's resolutions written and then stuck in a drawer will soon be forgotten. New Year's resolutions taped on the front of your refrigerator will not be forgotten.

Keep in close proximity those things on which you want to focus, and get all other distractions out of sight. You'll discover the power of proximity.

#46

TRANSITION TIME IS SELDOM MANAGED AND SO IMPORTANT!

Transition time is that time consumed as we move from one project to another, one meeting to another, or one activity to another. Basically, it's the time we spend disengaging from one activity and preparing to engage another.

Most people aren't aware of the time consumed in transitions. That's why managers often back one meeting up against the next, leaving no time to disengage from the last and go to the next. Here are three tips on managing transition time.

1. When scheduling meetings, be sure to schedule adequate transition time between them.

2. Say no to unnecessary interruptions. Considering the transition time involved with each interruption, it can take two to three times as long to recover from an interruption as it does to experience it.

3. Finally, develop an awareness of when you are in transition and not fully engaged or focused on anything.

IT'S DINNER TIME

Those were words everybody looked forward to hearing several decades ago when life moved at a slower pace. Unfortunately, dinner time has become one of the casualties of modern society and poor time management.

Taking time to sit down together as a family can pay huge relationship dividends. Sitting down together with your partner, your child, or your friend can truly be quality time.

Why not set a goal right now for some dinner time this month? Mark it on your calendar and enjoy far more than just good food.

#48

BECOME A DEDICATED NOTE TAKER TO SAVE TIME

Use a memory bucket (daily journal) where you note information you'll need at some time in the future. Avid note-taking saves time in a number of ways, including eliminating the need to check back with people and eliminating the fear of forgetting things. It also eliminates misunderstandings that might consume time.

#49

DO YOU SUFFER FROM FPAA?

FPAA is floating paper anxiety attack! It's caused by writing important messages on scraps of paper, yellow stickies, business cards, the backs of cash register receipts and who knows what all. The paper is easily lost; it mysteriously floats away. Then up goes anxiety. The information is important and time is wasted trying to get it again.

The solution is simple. Use the catch-all space in bucket two. Use one place to record information tidbits. When floating paper is handed to you, write the information in your "one place' in your time management tool. We get enough stress from outside sources; no need to do it to ourselves.

TIME SPONGES ARE COSTLY

A sponge soaks up water. A time sponge soaks up time that could otherwise be applied more effectively. There are three kinds of time sponges.

1. **Others** that soak up our time

2. **Habits** that soak up our time

3. **Problems** that soak up out time

The first kind, **others,** is controlled with discipline. The second kind, **habits,** is controlled with awareness and discipline. The third kind, **problems,** is controlled with anticipation and preparation.

Discipline, awareness, anticipation and preparation are essential skills for today's environment. Spot the sponges that are soaking up your time. Deal with that other person, that time-wasting habit, and anticipate problems in advance. You'll probably discover you'll have far more time than you think for the important things.

#51

PLAYING TAG AS A CHILD WAS FUN. TELEPHONE TAG IS NOT!

For sure, playing telephone tag is a time-waster. So why play? Make a change by setting telephone appointments and honoring them. If you can't take the time to talk with somebody who just called you, say so and set an appointment to call them back, rather than just say, "I'll call you back."

When responding in voicemail, don't just leave a message—leave some best times to reach you. And above all, avoid irritating others by saying your number so fast it's hard to understand, forcing them to waste time by replaying your message over and over to get your number.

These simple tips not only save time, they are good manners.

#52

MEETING YOURSELF FACE TO FACE

We demonstrate what is truly important to us by how we actually spend our time. When there is a disconnection between what we say is important and what we do with our time, we need to take a reality check. The reality may be uncomfortable, but it is true. We vote on what is honestly important to us with our time.

We invite you to look at your calendar and appointment schedule for the last three months. What does the record say about your priorities? If you are not pleased with the story it tells, make the necessary adjustments and align your time with what really matters to you.

A FIRE IS NOT AN INTERRUPTON OF A FIRE-FIGHTER'S WORK

Early in my career, I recall complaining about having too many fires to put out, to which my boss replied, "If you didn't have them, you wouldn't have a job." Enough said! I discovered four ways to not stress over interruptions that are necessary.

First, I changed my mind. I chose to see these things as the reason for my job, not interruptions of my job.

Second, I learned to anticipate the fires. I wrote "responding" next to the action list item and often prioritized it as a red.

Third, I learned to say "no" emphatically to issues that others could and should resolve themselves.

Fourth, I added every fire I put out to my list of accomplishments for the day. This helped replace my stress with high self-esteem and a sense of accomplishment.

Why not give these four ideas a try? If you stress over fighting a fire you were hired to put out, you are doing it to yourself.

#54

A MERCHANDISING TACTIC CAN BE USED AS A TIME TACTIC

A tip my Dad taught me when I worked as fashion buyer is simple but extremely helpful. Entering the sales room of a vendor could be intimidating and confusing with so many styles from which to choose.

He would challenge me by asking, "If you could buy only one item in this room, what would it be? What would be the most profitable?"

Once I made the choice, the next question was "If you could buy a second item what would it be?" When facing so many daily choices about where to invest your time, use the merchandising tactic. If you could do only one thing today, what would it be? Knowing the answer will help you to make the most relevant choices. It's a sensible choice-making tactic.

AN OPEN DOOR POLICY IS DIFFERENT FROM AN OPEN CLOCK POLICY

An open door policy means you are accessible by appointment. An open clock policy means you are accessible regardless of the time of day.

Time managers who grant access to themselves at any old time of day for any old issue not only don't get their own work done, but they don't grow people.

Be accessible, yes, but not too accessible. Guard your time and teach others to think for themselves.

#56

ARE YOU A TIMELY CONCLUDER?

When business is concluded and social etiquette has been expressed, it's time to move on.

Make it a point to exit meetings promptly. Avoid lingering on the telephone. Discipline yourself to not hover over email. Keep short discussions from evolving into office gossip.

Being slow to conclude is a hidden time-waster that washes more time down the drain than most people realize. Maintain a formal professional stance and use closure statements to disengage in a timely way, using your own style. Prepare closing statements in advance. Get good at using them, and you'll end up with a lot more time to do what counts.

ARE YOU PUTTING THE CART BEFORE THE HORSE?

A harried executive who was talking with us recently said, "I need to find time to arrange my time." People operating in this state are reaping the problems of putting the cart before the horse.

In this case, the cart is filled with the day's work-load, and the horse is time and energy essential in carrying the load. Nobody would ever really put a cart in front of the horse. On the other hand, many executives do something similar. They don't take sufficient time to arrange their time.

Devoting time to prioritize every day will get time pulling for you, not against you. We all need as much horse power "Time Power" as we can get.

#58

AVOID PROBLEMS – CLARIFY THE UNCLEAR

What does a person do if his or her role is unclear? Not much! What does a person do if instructions are unclear? Makes mistakes! What is the result of fuzzy communication? Misunderstanding!

Yes, failure to clarify the unclear is a serious TIME WASTER with negative consequences. Make certain when communicating to get feedback on what you said. The time required to clarify the unclear is minimal compared to the problems it solves. Don't forget to make notes on what it is you said.

#59

SLOW DOWN, YOU MOVE TOO FAST

One of the most enjoyable time management tips is to slow things up. People who are so rushed that they think they don't have time to take lunch or breaks should be given a warning rather than a badge of courage. It's unhealthy!

An internal combustion engine is not efficient if it's constantly running on full throttle, and neither is a human being. Schedule time for a relaxed lunch or an unrushed break. When you do, you'll discover you will operate more efficiently.

#60

BEWARE OF TIME BANDITS

Time bandits hold us up by making us wait. Time bandits are people who hold us up by asking "got a minute?" and then take ten.

- They hold us up with frequent overlong calls and unnecessary drop in visits.

- They hold us up by showing up late for meetings.

- They hold us up in hallways when we are trying to get someplace else.

Time bandits steal our time with office gossip. One time bandit, who takes fifteen minutes of our time daily, robs us of ninety hours per year. Remember, time bandits can't take your time unless you give it to them.

CAUTION! BEWARE OF THE EXPANSION EFFECT

Unless we are careful, work does expand to fill time allotted. Clutter does expand to fill the space available. And, even worse, commitments expand beyond the time available to do them. The net effect on the time manager is stress and guilt.

Guilt and stress don't have to happen. Here are two suggestions. Write down in one central place every obligation or commitment you make, and the time it will require. Take a few minutes each week to do a reality check of your promises, and cut back if necessary.

#62

CLUTTER IS THE WAKE OF RUNNING RUSHED

A messy office and desk top, a disorganized residence, and the general chaos of clutter is often the result of being frantically behind schedule. Consequently, there is no time to put files and physical objects back where they belong. Things are left out or tossed here and there and become harder to find the next time.

Get ahead of the game. Plan on the front end how much time your activities will take, and you'll reduce stress on the back end. You'll have time to put things away and save tons of time by not having to search for things. It can be done. Work to develop the habit and "mess stress" will be gone!

DECISIONS ARE FOOTPRINTS

Decisions are footprints we leave in the sands of time. We are remembered by the impressions we make in the lives of others, created with the use of our time. We cannot escape decisions. To not decide is a decision. Each decision leaves an impression. Our decisions are marked with each tick of the clock!

What is the point? Decisions create our legacy. Positive decisions move us and others forward. Negative decisions hold us back and can hurt others.

We complete our legacy with the impressions made with our time. Think!

#64

DON'T WISH YOUR TIME AWAY

This is often what my Mother said to me when I wished I was a little older, out of school, or had challenges behind me. From experience, I later learned she was right. Whether we have a fixation on future time or past time, the result is the same. We miss the good things about our present time.

The skill of focusing on and living in the present is one way to cherish time. Unfortunately, it is not practiced by many until they are older and see their time running out. Look for the good in your garden of today's time. It's there to be relished.

FAILSAFE GOAL GETTING

For most people, the start of a new year is received with positive anticipation. To use typical jargon, it's time to turn over a new leaf, make resolutions, get a fresh start, chart a new course or, in other words, begin anew.

Unfortunately, for many, dreams soon vaporize and resolutions die in the top dresser drawer. That won't happen to you this year if you use our power goal formula technique.

The power goal formula is simple and can serve as success insurance. Simply have fun using these ten power tips.

1. **Singularize it.** Pick one single goal that will enrich your life.

2. **Energizer it.** Make sure it is connected to an important innermost value.

3. **Write it.** Describe your goal in one specific sentence.

4. **Sub-divide it.** Build a pathway of written action steps that will get you there.

5. **Price it.** Ask, "Am I willing to pay the price?" If you really are, then proceed.

6. **Access it.** Constantly remind yourself of your goal by keeping it visually accessible on the refrigerator door, in your computer, in your wallet or posted in your workspace.

7. **Publish it.** Share your goal with others who will support you and hold you accountable.

8. **Visualize it.** Create a mind picture of your success, and visualize it when you get up in the morning and before you retire.

9. **Affirm it.** Make verbal success affirmations out loud each time you brush your teeth, and several times during the day.

10. Celebrate it. When you get there, savor your success and have a party. Email us your story so we that we can share with and inspire others. Email it to: goals@attackyourday.com.

GROUPING GETS MORE DONE

It's a fact that when people group like projects and do them all at once they tend to be more productive. Think about it! It takes less time to do six of the same things than six different things.

Practice this principle and it will spike your productivity.

#67

HOW IS YOUR TIME MANAGEMENT VISION?

For this test, don't just cover your left eye or your right eye: close both eyes. Now, visualize what specific and measurable things you will have accomplished between this moment and six months from now. Can you see the results you are anticipating clearly? If so, you have farsighted time management vision.

If you can't see what you will have accomplished, you are nearsighted. It is likely you are a reactive time manager and are working on the goals of others since you can't see your own. Is it time to write a goal-setting prescription to eliminate nearsightedness? Farsighted time managers actually write the scripts of their own lives.

HOW TO SUPERCHARGE YOUR DAILY ROUTINE

Most people aren't aware of this powerful time tactic! When you are listing high-priority tasks for the day, list a "personal principle" to practice. Some favorite principles of mine are being positive, praise others, smile, really listen and practice self-discipline.

Practice the personal principle you list all day long, then check it off complete at the end of the day as you would any other task.

You'll get progressively better at living the principle, impact others in a positive way, and feel better about yourself.

#69

IF EVERYTHING IS A PRIORITY, THEN NOTHING IS

Some people feel pushed to the limit with overwhelm. They see everything as an equally high priority. That's an illusion. An outstanding executive put it this way: "If everything is a priority, then nothing is." (Andrew Komenek.)

Survival today requires the skill of selecting the highest of high priorities in a mire of multiple demands. See through a lens of filter questions. Strengthen your **priority-eyes**. Here are three good questions that can be used any time of day: What things are absolute necessities today? If I don't do this today, who will it affect and who will suffer? What can I eliminate to free up more time?

BAD MOODS ARE
BIG TIME WASTERS

All of us are entitled to be upset and temporarily knocked off track by bad news, negative people and challenging situations. Serious time managers learn to snap back fast rather than slip into a prolonged time-wasting bad mood or even depression.

How do they do it? First, they recognize the condition is not worth a colossal drain of energy and time.

Next, they practice their own trigger technique to manage their mood. Our own technique is to recite this affirmation:

- I never let a **situation**…

- I never let a **condition**…

- I never let **another person**…

- I never let **bad news**…

- I never let **negative head talk** control my attitude.

"I choose my attitude." When conscious effort is made to control attitudes, most people are amazed at how much control they have and how much time they save.

WHEN TIME WINDOWS CLOSE

A time window is a period of time that brings with it an opportunity. Once that window is closed, the opportunity is lost. For example, an elderly couple regrets not traveling while they still had good health. Or, parents look back with sorrow because they didn't play with and enjoy their children while they were young.

When time windows slam shut and we didn't live the opportunities, we experience time remorse. Good time managers live the windows of opportunities and end up with great memories. "Memories are times that you borrow to spend when you get to tomorrow" (from Paul Anka's song Times of Your Life).

Are you looking at a time window soon to close? Is it time to make a memory?

#72

THE NINETY DAY ADVANTAGE

Most long-range planning doesn't work. The farther out we plan, the less likely the event is going to occur.

Try setting goals with ninety-day deadlines. You'll find ninety days is far enough out to succeed with many goals, but close enough in to motivate you to get started.

TIME TRACKING

Those who track their time control their time. Those who aren't time trackers don't control their time.

Use a planner, keep an appointment schedule, list what you plan to attack and then check off what you've completed. Presto! You'll be in control.

#74

SELF-DELEGATION IS A TIME TACTIC MANY OVERLOOK

We know delegating to others improves efficiency, but so does delegating to ourselves.

How do we delegate to ourselves? Batch a bunch of like tasks that you would delegate to another if you could, such as processing mail, filing, or other busy work. Schedule a specific time period to get it done and grind it out at that reserved time. Make a game of it! See how fast you can do it. It's amazing how much can be accomplished when we delegate to ourselves.

TIME MANAGEMENT SECRET – KEEP YOUR WEIGHT ON YOUR DOWNHILL SKI

When learning to ski, there is a natural tendency to recoil uphill away from the intimidating steep slope with weight on the uphill ski, rather than on the downhill ski. This causes the skier to lose control.

The same challenge occurs in time management. There is a natural tendency to recoil and lean away from tasks that intimidate us. One example would be a difficult call that needs to be made. Control your fear. Lean into and get your weight on the intimidating task. It will put you in control and you will not be a procrastinator.

RECOVERY TAKES TIME

Remember, there are three parts to the tasks we are managing. They are: WIND UP, EXECUTION, and WIND DOWN.

Many underestimate the time required to accomplish something because they plan time only for the execution of the task. They don't anticipate the time required for the wind up and wind down components.

SPONTANEOUS GOALS

A spontaneous goal is to execute an unplanned specific task on the spur of the moment. The best time to do this is when our environment presents us with a high-priority unexpected opportunity. Seize that opportunity and execute a spontaneous goal. *Spontaneous goals are not to be confused with being driven off-task by trivial, unexpected opportunities.*

People who practice spontaneous goals effectively often amaze others with how much they accomplish. What's more important, they often amaze themselves.

Source: Charles R. Hobbs

#78

TIME IS NOT REFUNDABLE

When we make a bad purchase with money, sometimes our money is refundable. When we make a bad investment of time, it is never refundable.

So time really isn't money, is it? It is more valuable than money and when it is spent, it is spent. Plan your time investments carefully.

#79

IS SOMETHING HANGING OVER YOUR HEAD?

I often hear people say, "I've got too much hanging over my head." When somebody says that, you know their energy is being drained. The longer something hangs up there, the heavier it feels. Energy that could be used to accomplish things is burned up in one's stress generator.

If something is hanging over your head and it's bothering you that means it's important! It's also likely it's hanging up there on the hooks of fear and indecisiveness. Postponement will only make things worse.

Lighten your load with three steps. First, determine the fear that's blocking you and face it. Second, decide when and how you'll get it done. Third, do it.

The relief you'll feel will far outweigh the challenge of getting it done.

WALK AWAY TIME

A good time management skill is to recognize when it's time to walk away from something! Perhaps you've been sitting at your desk and the ideas just aren't coming. Maybe your effectiveness is diminished due to an energy drain or lack of clarity. When you feel you are in such a state, recognize it, stop what you are doing, walk away and do something else. Failure to do so wastes time!

On a larger scale, have the courage to not continue to ride "dead horse" projects. Knowing when to walk away is a big time saver.

A TIME MANAGEMENT CODE OF CONDUCT

1. I never hold others hostage by keeping them waiting. I call, and inform people if I am going to be late.

2. I arrive at meetings a few minutes early and prepared.

3. I don't text or read email while talking face to face to somebody.

4. I never send non-essential email.

5. I never keep others waiting for information needed to complete their own projects on time.

6. I acknowledge calls in a timely way and never ignore people.

7. I'm careful not to exceed the number of minutes others allocate to me.

8. I never barge into another's work space without asking to come in.

9. I encourage others to get their fair share of talk time in meetings.

10. I never waste the time I'm being paid to use.

11. I keep my promise to call people back.

12. I don't waste time on office gossip.

13. I avoid making overlong phone calls and unnecessary drop in visits.

14. I don't ask people if they've got a minute and then take fifteen minutes.

15. I always thank others for their time.

NO DOOR ON YOUR OFFICE?

An aura is defined as, "a distinctive atmosphere surrounding a given source." Many are not aware they create their own time management aura that is easily picked up by others. Fortunately, we can create any aura we desire.

Create an aura that telegraphs the feeling that you value your own time and the time of others. When you do, you will increase respect from others and reduce interruptions from others. When you don't have a door on your office, an aura can perform a similar function.

An aura is built by indirectly training others in your time management style by how you respond to them. For example, immediately rescheduling drop-in visitors on the spot rather than accommodating them. This telegraphs a powerful message that your space is personal and carefully guarded.

#83

ARE YOU AN INSENSITIVE OR SENSITIVE TIME MANAGER?

We receive telephone calls from two types of callers: the sensitive and the insensitive.

After we answer the telephone, **insensitive** callers barge right into a conversation and jabber away as though no matter what we are doing, their issue is more important. Never mind the fact that we just hit our stride on a project, or just stepped out of the shower.

Sensitive callers recognize they are interrupting and are careful to first get permission to proceed. They say something like "I hope I didn't catch you at a bad time" or, "I'm sorry for the interruption, do you have time for a question?"

Demonstrating to others we are sensitive about their time is the mark of a professional.

#84

THE THREE STAGES OF INTERRUPTIONS

It has been traditional in the time management business to say it takes three times as long to recover from an interruption as it takes to experience it. This is due in large part to the three stages of responding.

First, there is wind down time, which drops the effectiveness level on which you were working. Then there is resolution time, which is the time devoted to dealing with the interruption. Next, there is wind up time, the time necessary to get you back up to the level on which you were working. The clock keeps ticking throughout these three stages, and more time is consumed than most people realize.

#85

THE LONG AND SHORT OF TIME MANAGEMENT

Many people never achieve what they want with their time. The reason is not making the connection between the long and short of time management. The long of time management is desired future outcomes. The short of time management is today's actions.

How does one make the connection between the long and short of time? It's achieved by connecting the two with the *coupler of clarity*. Determine clearly what future outcome is desired and clarify the short-term steps needed to make it happen. Then, make sure your daily actions are some of the steps connected to your desired future. Have you taken the time to connect the long and short of it all?

SLICE YOUR TIME LIKE PIE

Most people cut an hour of time into quarters, but time breaks down more efficiently into ten-minute periods. We have six ten-minute slices of time to invest each hour.

Think in terms of ten-minute increments of time when planning and budgeting activities. Much can be accomplished in a ten-minute slice of time. You can return a call, write a letter, file some documents, resolve an issue, clear some email, and on and on.

Become a ten-minute manager and you will become an effective time manager. "Many a great man has snatched his reputation from odd bits of time which others, who wonder at their failure, throw away" (unknown).

SCHEDULE A RACE AGAINST TIME

So you find yourself slipping into preoccupation? Does it take longer to do the work you have to do than it should? Are you too slow getting started? Is your energy low?

Schedule a race with time and you can temporarily fix all of the problems above. It's easy! Simply decide on the task or tasks you want to get done. Give yourself a start time and an ending time that will make you stretch, then get started on your race with the clock. If anybody tries to interrupt you say, "Hey I'm timing this."

Make activity management fun. Make a game of it. You'll probably surprise yourself at how much you can accomplish in shorter time periods. Why not schedule at least one race against time this week?

USE BURSTS OF EFFORTS FOR BETTER TIME MANAGEMENT

I read this quotation the other day, on a blog posted by Michael Wade. "We plan our day as if we work in a steady flow but we really work in bursts of activity."

Once an activity manager embraces that principle, it can be leveraged for richer, more satisfying time utilization, and of course, higher productivity.

How do we leverage this principle? Attack each task with a burst of concentrated effort, followed by a different task that uses a different set of mental and physical muscles. This will give you a chance to recover. Then, attack the next more difficult task with another "burst." It's a very comfortable way to get things done!

#90

WHERE YOUR TIME GOES, THERE ARE YOUR TRUE PRIORITIES

Time flows toward what people feel is important, not what they say is important. It's an uncomfortable reality to recognize that what we do with our time validates what we want from our time.

When we say something or someone is important, but it isn't matched with proportional time, the message is clear. When we say something is not important, but it's getting a lot of our time, the message is also clear. We show the world everyday what is truly important to us by what activities we choose to do.

We can re-direct the course of our day at any point by re-focusing on our most important activities.

80% OF TIME MANAGEMENT PROBLEMS ARE SELF-IMPOSED!

Many feel that eighty percent of their time management problems come from others when, in reality, eighty percent are self-imposed.

There are at least twenty self-imposed habits that cannibalize time. Here are four examples: unwilling to say no, attempting too much, procrastination, and insufficient planning. Do you own any of these?

The good news is we can control self-imposed time wasters with practice and discipline. Remember what we were told as children: "When we point our finger at somebody else, there are four pointing back at us."

Control the four time wasters mentioned above and other self imposed problems, and you'll be an incredible time manager. Then other people won't be your problem!

NOISE POLLUTERS ARE THE NEW AGE TIME ROBBERS

Noise polluters shout into their cell phones in restaurants, on commercial transportation and in open office environments. Sometimes they even do this while sitting right next to somebody. They set the ringers on their phones loud enough to serve as fire alarms, and their bizarre ring styles become further distractions. They don't seem to care at all for those around them.

Distractions interrupt others, intrude into their time space, and make it difficult to concentrate. Promote a healthy time environment. Eliminate cell phone noise pollution. It is common courtesy.

JUST IN TIME, TIME MANAGEMENT

There is a huge population out there that postpones getting started on important projects. Putting themselves under the gun creates pressure. Pressure often unleashes our productivity and creative juices. Tight deadlines jolt us into action!

People often apologize that they do this, but it does work for many. We suggest it be used in moderation as a periodic technique. Fight the urge to use it as a crutch every time. Instead, do a little something on the project every day. That way you'll reduce stress, finish the project early, and get a rush of satisfaction.

Remember! The closer to the deadline, the more difficult it is to recover should something go wrong.

#94

WHAT IS THE BEST USE OF MY TIME RIGHT NOW?

A sensible swimmer always assesses the water before diving in. An astute time manager first pauses and looks at the sea of options before plunging into chaos.

Here then is an important time management technique. Before plunging, pause momentarily and ask the instant time management question. It is: "What is the best use of my time right now?" Decide what it is, then do that thing first. You can use this question many times during the day to keep from drowning in a sea of irrelevancy. Try it, you'll like it.

Source: Charles R. Hobbs, Time Power

#95

RUTS, ROUTINES, RITUALS AND YOUR TIME

Ruts are bad time management habits that should be eliminated. An example is preoccupation. Get out as fast as you can!

Routines are activities that need to be repeated on a daily, weekly, or monthly basis. Systemize these by determining the best times, places and methods for getting them done, then do them the same way every time. If you do, you'll be more efficient.

Rituals are personal techniques for putting yourself in the best state for accomplishing the tasks you are facing. An example is driving negative head talk out of your mind with positive affirmations. For example, "My presentation is going to go extremely well," repeated over and over again.

Analyze your ruts, routines and rituals. Get out of the ruts, streamline your routines, and create some rituals. The use of your time will be much more effective.

#96

THE MOST ANCIENT TIME MANAGEMENT TIP

It is: "Go to bed early and get up early." People who do this get the golden hour.

The golden hour is a quiet hour free of interruptions and distractions. It is a time when most are rested and mentally alert. Many people get three times the productivity out of a golden hour than from a typical hour at another time of day.

When others are just getting started, those who got a golden hour already have momentum. That is a darn good reason to be an early riser. Make it a habit to go for the gold.

TAKE A BREAK FROM TIME MANAGEMENT

Looking for answers? Too much structure and minute to minute intensity can actually shut down the creative portion of your brain from where answers come. Plant the question with which you are struggling in the back of your mind, and then forget it for a while. Lighten up and take some time off. Do something you really enjoy doing. Sleep on it.

As you relax, your subconscious will be freed up and keep working for you. The answer will come when you least expect it, sometimes at three in the morning. When it comes, write it down fast so it doesn't slip away.

#98

IS YOUR PROBLEM YOUR BOSS?

Over the years, I've had countless executives come up to me after workshops with the following question: "What do you do if your boss is your time management problem? He/she interrupts me all day long." My answer is: "You don't have a time management problem; you have a communication problem!" So, here's the tip.

When trying to find solutions to interruptions, first find the **underlying cause**. That includes your boss. Sit down with your boss, communicate and get it resolved. Another executive complained, "When others in the office go on vacation, my boss dumps all of their work on my desk. Then I can't get my own work done." My response was, "What is the underlying cause?" Clearly it was a lack of cross-functional training in the department.

Chronic interruptions, including those from your boss, are symptoms of deeper problems. That's why they can't be fixed with something as superficial as body language. Find the underlying causes of your interruptions, fix them, and the problems will disappear.

THE THREE-MINUTE HOUR

The three-minute hour is fun, fast and effective. You'll love it! Here's how it works. Set aside an hour in your office to not be interrupted. Get together every loose end you can think of that you can do in three minutes or less, and do them.

Focus on such things as notes you've made on little pieces of paper, short calls where people are waiting for a quick answer. File loose papers, make dinner reservations and any other activities you can do in three minutes or less. If it can't be done in three minutes or less, don't do it.

At the end of the hour, your loose ends will be done and you'll feel a great sense of accomplishment.

#100

FOUR WAYS ANY ORGANIZATION CAN INCREASE PRODUCTIVITY

Most would agree time is our most precious commodity. Why then do so many organizations pay so little attention to its use? Here are four things any organization can do to increase productivity:

1. Heighten the value of time in the minds of all members by talking about it in meetings and all areas of communication.

2. Teach time management skills to all members and require them to use a time management system.

3. Hold all persons accountable by measuring what is accomplished with their time.

4. Cut meeting time in half with better planning.

How does your organization measure up? Are you paying enough attention to its use?

TRAPPER'S WORK-LIFE MOTTO

Have Faith, it will sustain you

Plan Carefully, it's essential

Simply life, get rid of stuff

Lighten Your Load, toss mental baggage

Be Strong, because you are

Experience Nature, it's God's medicine

In memory of Trapper Woods
1935-2010

ATTACK YOUR DAY!
Before It Attacks You

www.attackyourday.com

We provide productivity tools and education to help individuals and corporations succeed in a chaotic work-life environment.

For More Information: call 888-972-0800 to learn how you can hire one of our certified trainers.

Other Books by Trapper Woods

Service! Some People Just Don't Get It! – *A Simple System to Make Your Customer Service Sizzle!*
Authors Trapper Woods and Todd Woods

Tick Tock! Who Broke the Clock? – *Solving the Work-Life Balance Equation*
Authors Trapper Woods and William Guillory

Order these books online at:
Amazon.com.

time4life

Time is our most precious commodity. In most cases it takes something of magnitude, like the diagnosis of cancer, disease or other traumatizing event to realize just how precious time really is.

I know because it happened to me. Three weeks after completing this book I lost my father Trapper Woods to cancer.

After twenty months of fighting the disease, he passed away on his 75th birthday. He committed 23 years of his life to the subject of time and work-life balance.

Mission To provide training resources to people that have been traumatized by diagnosis or illness.

Who it Supports Time 4 Life is a program for anyone directly or indirectly traumatized by diagnosis or illness that is overwhelmed and in need of time.

Get Involved Learn how you can get involved at our website www.time4life.org.

Mark Woods, Co-Author
Attack Your Day! Before It Attacks You

LaVergne, TN USA
22 March 2011
221101LV00003B/10/P